MOST BUSINESSES FAIL IN THE FIRST 5 MINUTES.

IT JUST TAKES THEM 3 TO 5 YEARS TO REALIZE IT.

Position to Win

Co-Conspirators:
John Paul Mendocha & Gabe Bautista

Volume One: The First Ace

ISBN: 978-1-933525-00-6

LCN: 2019916213

Published by Bleeding Neck, LLC

5605 Riggins Court, Suite 200, Reno, Nevada 89502

PositionToWinBook.com

Printed in the United States

Praise for *Most Businesses Fail in the First 5 Minutes*

"Over the last decade and a half, I've done a lot of in-person events with John Paul Mendocha. The guy is a hell of a storyteller. When he presents to Perry Marshall audiences, one thing is for sure: people either love him or they're horrified. But everyone learns something. Everyone.

For years his friends and I have been poking at him to get a book written. Get his crazy-ass stories into print. And he finally did it. He collaborated with Gabe Bautista (who is also a ball of fire) and now wider audiences everywhere can access these wild tales and smart insights.

I've worked with my share of business owners, and one thing is for damn sure: most of them did, in fact, fail in their first 5 minutes. They got their positioning all wrong. But that's what and who this book is for. It will set you straight on how to find your unique position in the market and how to get people, a lot of people, to suddenly perk up and give a genuine crap about you.

I especially liked the bit about Grandma's soup."

—Bryan Todd, President, Perry S. Marshall and Associates

"For years John Paul Mendocha has brought his special, hard-earned, and powerful wisdom to the savvy operators who attend my Black Ops seminars held in Tempe,

Arizona. Year after year those business and professional practice owners ask "When will John write a book?" Well, he's delivered and his new book *Most Businesses Fail in the First 5 Minutes: It Just takes Them 3 to 5 Years to Realize It,* will get you thinking in new and better ways. If you're like me you'll also wonder how and why you ever made those mistakes. But, thanks to John Paul you'll never make them again. Every business owner or entrepreneur should:

    1) grab a copy of this book and then

    2) plan to see John Paul Mendocha live."

—David M. Frees III JD, Creator and "The Old Man" at Business Black Ops

"As a psychologist, I know that much of what we understand about people comes from real-world observations, not academic studies. John Paul Mendocha has spent a lifetime observing and engaging with all kinds of people in all kinds of settings. And he shares his astute insights in his new book *Most Businesses Fail in the First 5 Minutes.*

In the commonsense and wry style, I've seen over years of knowing John Paul, he explains how to catch and make meaning from the subtleties in how people act that most of us miss. Then he shows you how to take that information and make faster and better decisions in business and in the rest of your life, too. If you haven't learned from him before, the book is time well spent. If you have learned from John Paul before, you'll find new insights in *Most Businesses Fail in the First 5 Minutes.*"

—David A. Weiman, Psy.D., Weiman Consulting

"John Paul Mendocha is the most captivating storyteller I have ever known: amazing, exciting. His stories are entertaining, and when there is money on the line, the stories are SOLID GOLD! As a manufacturer's rep and distributor for over 26 years in high tech, I can attest to the fact that the WINNERS got it, they thrived. Sadly, the losers desperately needed this book and slowly slipped into the morass. My only wish is that John Paul had written this when I was starting out. If you want to choose the winning path, you will devour this book. I have personally seen John Paul conjure sales magic and he has captured that lightening in this volume. Your task is to purchase anything he is offering—you will always be happy you did."

—Gerry Hauer, Entrepreneur, Force of Nature

"This book takes on a huge challenge. It unwraps and reveals the secrets of the first five minutes in a way everyone can understand, it reveals the secrets of positioning. You must read this book."

—Tom Meloche, co-author of *The Ultimate Guide to Facebook Advertising,* author of *Ceremony: A Profound New Method for Achieving Successful and Sustainable Change*

"Every business owner has a problem hidden in plain sight. This problem has existed since the beginning of time. The real problem, however, is actually knowing what the problem is. Usually, it's buried right in front of our very eyes. Until we figure out what it is, we can never really solve it. Some of us stumble upon solutions and find a way to get through it, but I've struggled with this my entire business life. Fortunately, there is a way forward. In fact, I found the way forward in reading *Most Businesses Fail in the First 5 Minutes.*

John Paul Mendocha and Gabe Bautista cut through the haze shining a light directly on the problem. Their process took me from the state of blissful ignorance to the heart of a universal problem I know will affect every single business owner, entrepreneur, and achiever who wants to improve their life. I highly recommend you take off the blindfold, put on the bright light, read this book, and skip right over the blissful ignorance phase. You'll be awakened, alive and ready for greater success."

—Frank F. Lunn, CEO, Kahuna Accounting
Dynamic Guidance Accounting for Growth Entrepreneurs

"John Paul Mendocha slams it out of the park on the first pitch with his acclaimed: *Most Business Fail in the First 5 Minutes* book. This book is jam-packed full of business fundamentals, yet has the depth of 400 graduate level sales and marketing courses, providing skills that will keep you re-reading it. I know, I've built a very successful sales career using these skills, and I'll be re-reading the book soon to gain even more fresh insights. Thanks John!"

—Murray Egan, Director of Sales, Integrity Security Services

"These concepts for me are like the last scene in the Matrix movie where Neo is able to see the numbers in the walls and realize that it is all a construct—being able to under-stand concepts like positioning or the adoption curve gives me the ability to see that actually, my business has been successful out of sheer luck but now to be able to see the dials and use them so that I can position myself effectively,"

—Dike Drummond MD, Doctor Burnout Master Coach

Praise for *Most Businesses Fail in the First 5 Minutes*

"Gabe and John Paul are spot on with this book. Starting off with the title *Most Business Fail in the First 5 Minutes*, spot on. I totally relate to it because it happened to me. It took me five years to get to the situation described in Chapter 13. I wish I would have read this book five years ago, it would have saved me a lot of heartache and uncertainty. This is your time, read it, soak it all in and position yourself to win. Thank you, Gabe, Thank you, John Paul. God bless you."

—María Tobelen, Entrepreneur, The Holistic Hypothyroid and Autoimmune Enlightener

"Grateful for what I have learned and been able to apply thus far. Because of these concepts in positioning I have been able to position my team for multi-million dollar projects that other people wanted to take credit for. I have used these lessons to be able to set our team up to be recognized but also to fend off others that would ordinarily take credit away."

—Doug Wesney, Senior Executive, Waste Management Company

"Thank you for the challenging and the provoking and the agitating of the different pain points that draw attention to what I really need to know and do in my business and the reality of it. I have been positioning myself by really embracing who I am, going on Facebook Live and speaking about what I think is important in Sales and in Closing. It has been almost cathartic, because I am talking about what I think people need to know, and by embracing that and who I am, together with my position, I am instantly different."

—Richard Duggal, Real Estate Team Building, Listing Machine and Closing Extraordinaire

"Whether you have a business or you're thinking about starting one, this book will help you avoid the most critical mistake most entrepreneurs make: They become number two! History has shown us through the centuries that nobody ever remembers who's gotten the number two position! So, what if you could create such powerful positioning in your niche and market that will make you #1 and eliminate your competition? This book will give you the insights to achieve just that! A must-read."

—Jose Luis Galvis, Entrepreneur, Leading Latin American Digital Marketing Authority"

"The fact that you guys were able to break down the sales process into a granular step by step idea is something I think every business owner should know and have awareness of. It has given me a lot of work to do but it has opened up my eyes to how I can scale what I have, and even do other things in business!"

—Luigi Gonzalez, Telecommunication Business Owner

"What this book did for me was that it took away a lot of the mystery of starting things up, showing that you can actually have direction and focused effort on what matters rather than just keeping your fingers crossed hoping everything works out. These are great insights on why things work out the way they do, and why things don't work out the way they do."

—Bill Farinella, Logistics Specialist and 3rd Generation PHVAC Business Expert

"*Most Businesses Fail in the First 5 Minutes* book is awesome. Easy to read and compelling enough to want to read more. John Paul did a great job on the red cover with the Success-O-Meter.

What really gives it the credibility it deserves is your research and examples. I especially love the quote 'How you view yourself versus how others view you is radically different.' John Paul, you have written a winner!"

—Trish MacDonald, Real Estate Professional Extraordinaire

"Want to boost your confidence? Tilt the odds in your favor? Succeed where others fail? For anyone in a sales career, positioning is one of the keys to success. *Most Businesses Fail in the First 5 Minutes* shows a salesperson how to identify and exploit their already existing talents. Then use those talents to put themselves (and product) in the best possible position in the mind of the client. Highly recommended!"

—Gary Schipporeit, Business Development Manager, Engineering

"Having helped incorporate over forty thousand businesses over my career, success makes my chest expand, and failures always bring a bit of sadness. *Most Businesses Fail in the First 5 Minutes* should help change the mix, creating more successes than failures. The odds are not stacked, only unknown. John Paul and Gabe have put forth a book that could turn the tide. Highly recommended."

—Trevor Rowley, Executive Vice President, Nevada Corporate Headquarters, Inc.

Dedication

To my wife, Rebecca and my brother, Michael—the two pocket Aces of my life. Through it all you have always been there. If I were to believe in luck, you both would be the proof of its existence.

John Paul Mendocha

Dedicado a los que siempre creyeron en mí inclusive cuando ni yo mismo creía. Ustedes saben quienes son, y yo también. Los quiero.

Gabriel Bautista

Table of Contents

Table of Contents

Rules of Position to Win

1. Most businesses fail in the first five minutes.
2. It just takes them three to five years to realize it.
3. All positioning begins with you.
4. You can't occupy two positions at the same time.
5. Perception is reality.
6. Logic plus emotion equals *bias*.
7. Selling prevention is nearly impossible.
8. Where are you on the Adoption Curve?
9. Don't think you can escape, we all have the rock in the shoe syndrome.
10. A confused mind always says, "No."
11. Denial of your own position is an outright losing proposition.
12. If caught with seven Aces in a poker game, feign surprise.
13. If you're waiting for an original idea, you have missed the point.
14. The Sharp Edge of Marketing is the personification of a bias map.
15. Play the hand that is in front of you.
16. Would somebody please shut up that damn coyote!
17. Avoid the brown M&M's—they are bad mojo.

Foreword

It is a bold proposition to say that "most businesses fail in the first five minutes." If you are a first time entrepreneur the statement may even raise your inner skeptic, you may find yourself asking "Can it be true? Are the first five minutes really that important?"

Those of us who see being an entrepreneur as a calling, eventually come to realize the truth of the statement. Even if we have never before put it into words. I've personally been involved in over a dozen startups, some which were acquired, some which went public, some which still run, and others which went beautifully bankrupt. Yes, most businesses fail in the first five minutes. This is simultaneously a universally understood truth, and an unspoken secret.

Entrepreneurs are eternal optimists, living in our imagination. Literally imaging things into existence. And, unlike the politician who uses the threat of violence to impose their will, entrepreneurs use customer satisfaction. The customer is the beginning and end of our existence. And the customer, through a choice of their own free will, provides us custom. There is a reason many of us entrepreneurs consider entrepreneurship to be the highest calling, and the highest achievement, in all of human history. Entrepreneurs have been infinitely more successful than any other class at actually ending disease, want, and human suffering, all through the force of our imagination.

The challenge is, our entire existence is dependent on customer choice, free will, how our customers perceive us, and not how we perceive ourselves. This is true for all entrepreneurial endeavors.

Not realizing our entire existence begins and ends entirely by how customers perceive us is very very costly. And this, this positioning, is what almost everyone gets wrong in the first five minutes. Very few businesses survive this mistake.

This book takes on a huge challenge. It unwraps and reveals the secrets of the first five minutes in a way everyone can understand, it reveals the secrets of positioning. You must read this book.

Some people, and I include myself among them, are addicted to reading business books, I have even written a few. Business flows in our blood. Entrepreneurs and business leaders are our heroes. And not just the big entrepreneurs, all entrepreneurs: the small restaurateur, the coffee shop owner, and a startup in a big city delivering plants door-to-door. All of them heroes. And heroes whether they succeed or fail. But... if we are going to put in all this effort, why not succeed?

Very few business books, however, help us survive the First Five Minutes. I can think of only one, and you are holding it.

I haven't been as excited about a new business book in years. So here is my suggestion... get your business partners and team together and set aside 10 minutes a day for the next two to three weeks. Each day someone reads a chapter out loud to the team, as a team activity. Do the exercises and discuss them. Do this until you know, truly know, you are positioned to win.

—Tom Meloche, **BCE in Electrical and Computer Engineering, co-author of** *The Ultimate Guide to Facebook Advertising,* **author of** *Ceremony: A Profound New Method for Achieving Successful and Sustainable Change,* Co-Founder of Menlo Innovations, company featured in Joy Inc., Master of Space, Time and Industry

Ann Arbor, Michigan, September 22, 2019

Who is Tom Meloche?

The entertainment industry would have you believe that entrepreneurs look act and talk a specific way. This judge-a-book-by-it's-cover approach stands in stark contrast to the many entrepreneurs working the soil to spring their ideas to life. When asked about the thinness of the wrapper of a Snickers bar, Forrest Mars said, "They don't eat the wrapper."

As I got to know Tom Meloche, that statement could not be truer. In fact, he is an incredible software luminary who stumbled into this quirky world known as Internet marketing and was one of the early conquerors of Facebook advertising. Years ahead of anyone that I knew at the time, and still beyond most of the pack, I recognized him as someone from one of those '50's B movies where there was always the evil scientist holed up in a hollowed out volcano with lots of laboratory equipment, flashing lights and swirling discs.

Tom exhibits amazing insights into not only how to construct software, but through his work in *Ceremony*, brings counterintuitive approaches to a world that is often reactionary. When I asked him to write this foreword, he said, "I'll be happy to, but it may take a while." I couldn't be more pleased with the result.

—John Paul Mendocha

Introduction

Deal Yourself a Winning Hand

During the 1994 movie Maverick, starring Mel Gibson as Bret Maverick, the actors are in the final hand of a high-stakes poker tournament. Remaining at the table are James Coburn, who plays Commodore Duvall, the dealer, and another actor with slicked back hair, a dark brown handle bar mustache and trail-hardened face who sits across the table from Maverick.

Bret has looked at his hand except for one card. That card is face down on the table. Handlebar glares at Maverick, "How are you gonna know if you can beat my straight flush?" He lays down a heart flush to the seven.

The commodore stares in disbelief, because that beat his four of a kind and he chomps hard on his cigar in disgust. The crowd gasps, then cheers, claps, and laughs. One man quips, "Unbeatable."

Everyone looks to Bret. He puts down his first card. "The ten of spades," calls out the dealer. The second card: "The jack of spades." Then, "Queen of spades. The king of spades. A possible royal flush."

A roar goes up from the crowd. "Quiet. Quiet."

Bret puts his hand above the unknown card on the table. He flexes his fingers, almost afraid to even touch the card. He looks at Handlebar who is intensely glaring at him.

He picks up the card without looking at it. He is still staring at his opponent. Is he going to be lucky? Is he going to win or is he going to fail yet again? Life changes rest with this one card. Everyone wants to win. Life is always about winning. The spoils go to the winners.

Bret's eyes move downward to the card in his hand. He glances at it. His face falls. The crowd groans. He gives a big sigh and drops his shoulders. Then he flings the card out over the table and it lands face up on the gold pile of chips. The Ace of spades.

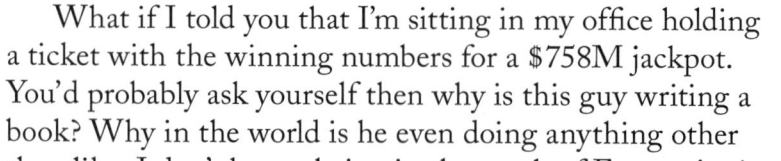

If winning scares you don't read another word.

Everyone wants a winning hand. Everyone wants the royal flush while playing poker. The odds of it are 649,739 to 1.

———— ◆ ————

What if I told you that I'm sitting in my office holding a ticket with the winning numbers for a $758M jackpot. You'd probably ask yourself then why is this guy writing a book? Why in the world is he even doing anything other than like, I don't know, being in the south of France, jetting around the world, picking out my new Rolls-Royce.

The point is you can have the winning numbers. In fact, I have the winning number for the second largest lottery jackpot in U.S. history. The problem is, it's not the right date. The numbers, by the way are: 6, 7, 16, 23, and

26. The Powerball number is 4. That isn't the issue. The problem is that my ticket says June 19, 2019. The winning ticket was purchased for the Powerball that took place on August 23, 2017.

See, here's the catch about lotteries. You have to have the right numbers on the right day. Now maybe if I could go back in time, use a DeLorean and hit 88 miles an hour, and buy this ticket at that point in time, then I too could have the winning lottery ticket. The realization is that every time there is a lottery, you have a two-step process. And it's simple:

1. Select the correct numbers.

2. Select the correct date.

Easy to do—easy to say; almost impossible to accomplish. Anybody can go buy the right numbers, but it's making sure you do it on the correct day. By the way, on that August 23, 2017, a person walked into who-knows-where in Massachusetts, bought a single ticket, and won that jackpot. Lottery fever was all around.

Millions were waiting in line to buy tickets, fantasizing about what they were going to do with the money. All those people actually had two problems. They may have had the right day, but they didn't have the right numbers, or vice versa, or they didn't have either.

Life is filled with the type of situation where you need all the pieces of the puzzle to fit together. The Powerball odds which are even higher than poker at 281,000,000 to 1, still get people lining up to buy tickets! Maybe playing the Powerball isn't the best strategy for your retirement.

I'm holding that winning ticket right now. I just need to have the right date come up again. But, of course, that is sheer fantasy. Part of life is understanding that the lottery is not a strategy; it is a guess, it's a hope, it's a prayer. In fact, it's been deemed a tax on the poor, naive and stupid.

I'm going to hold on to this ticket, because I know, in my heart of hearts, that I bought a winning ticket. And if I could just go back in time, I would split a $758M jackpot. Don't be deluded by such fantasy. That is not a strategy for success.

Knowing the winning lottery numbers would be great. But the problem is that you don't. Even getting the right numbers a day late won't get you any kind of recognition.

You need the right numbers at the right time.

Now there is a metaphor for life!

Winning numbers for $758 Million. Note to self:
Go back in time and play these numbers.

Why Winning is so Important

If you don't win, come in first, be ahead of all the others, then you have a serious drop in your self-confidence which leads to a loss in your self-esteem. The reason why winning is so important is that it is the winners, those who get to that first place, who garner most of the rewards. It is an application of the 80/20 principle, The 80/20 principle is dis-equal distribution of results.

There are those who believe that this is a percentages game that you can play. They believe that deferring (losing) is just another step towards success and winning, There are many motivational speakers and feel-good charlatans who believe in the gambler's fallacy historically known as the maturity of chances, which states that all you have to do is keep playing and you must eventually win. Not on this planet.

The maturity of chances is a fallacy. This reality keeps entrepreneurs that have already failed in the first 5 minutes alive and marching for the next 3 to 5 years, to a place they're never going to get to.

All the 0's are losing. All the 1's are winning. You can't win them all—recognizing that some hands are unwinnable, some are improvable and some are undefeatable. Win, lose or draw you have to play each hand to the best of your ability.

In reality, those who win, well, they get one hundred percent. Those who lose get zero, zilch, nada, cero pollito. Everybody behind the winner are all losers.

Watch something like the Indianapolis 500 and you'll see that in over 500 miles the margin of victory is measured in less than a few seconds and sometimes in hundredths of a second. What a dramatic difference between being the winner versus number two, being the first loser, and everyone behind you losing even more so.

So winning isn't everything, but it is significantly more important than most people understand. For 2019, I saw Simon Pagenaud beat the 2016 Indy winner, Alexander Rossi, by 0.2086 of a second.

OFFICIAL BOX SCORE
NTT INDYCAR SERIES
103rd Indianapolis 500 presented by Gainbridge
May 26, 2019

FP	SP	Car	Driver	Car Name	Laps	Reason Out	Pts	Total Pts	Standings	Earnings
1	1	22	Simon Pagenaud	Menards Team Penske Chevrolet	200	Running	112	250	1	$2,669,529
2	9	27	Alexander Rossi	NAPA AUTO PARTS Honda	200	Running	82	228	3	$759,179
3	14	30	Takuma Sato	Mi-Jack / Panasonic Honda	200	Running	71	203	4	$540,454
4	8	2	Josef Newgarden	Shell V-Power Nitro Plus Team Penske Chevrolet	200	Running	67	249	2	$462,904
5	6	12	Will Power	Verizon 5G Team Penske Chevrolet	200	Running	65	184	6	$444,554

Indy 500 Official Box Score, May 26, 2019

Rossi went on to say,

> **"But unfortunately, nothing else matters here but winning. This one will be hard to get over, but at the end of the day, it was a great showing for the team and good for the points overall. But today will suck for a while."**

Simon Pagenaud earned $2.669 million dollars for coming in number one, Alexander Rossi earned $759,000 for second place, a difference of about $1.9 million.

The reason *Most Businesses Fail in the First 5 Minutes* came about was the realization that everyone must start to think in terms of how do I put myself in the most favorable position to win more often than I lose. How do I get to that point where I have the odds in my favor so that I am able to enjoy the benefits of winning?

That winning builds upon itself, there is a positive momentum, there is a sense of assuredness, a confidence that grows. People want to hear from winners. People want to talk to winners. People know that those who are in authority have won something, are standing out above everyone else. Make no mistake, this is a very competitive world.

> The meek shall inherit the earth, but not its mineral rights.
> —J. Paul Getty

There's Never a Crowd Around the Loser's Circle

Now, this flies in the face of current thinking and current ways to operate, but this will not change reality and human nature. We have been competitive since the very beginning. The first cave man walked into the communal cave, beat soundly on his chest and bellowed to his next door neighbor, "Me beat you at throwing stones tonight." To which the second cave man growled, "You are nuts. It's never gonna happen. Game on!"

No matter what school of thought you adhere to, no matter how far back you go, the winners, those who persevered, those who forged ahead, are the ones who successfully advanced. Our distant relatives, those who survived and moved this species forward, were the winners. Rarely, if ever, do the losers get any recognition at all, and are forgotten almost instantly.

Winning is highly significant; but why is it so important? If you can develop a winning mind-set and position yourself to win every day, in the end you will be significantly more successful than all of the other losers out there.

Can You Handle the Truth?

> The future always arrives on time. Nothing else is guaranteed, including who among us will be here to greet it and what will stock its shelves.
> —Bob Greene

Many people believe different things about what makes someone more or less successful. Is it Intelligence? Is it your DNA? What percentile IQ do you fall into?

Maybe what determines if someone is successful is education. Perhaps what you need is a Harvard MBA. As of November 5, 2018, according to Forbes, a Harvard MBA costs a cool $213,600 plus other costs; never mind what it takes to get accepted to Harvard. It's really difficult because only about 9.4% of applicants attain that status, and out of the roughly 330 million people in the U.S., that's .00000303% who make it. Those are tough odds.

> **If I had chosen my parents,
> I would have been a billionaire right now.**
>
> **—Marc Hammer, Bankrate Senior Analyst**

Maybe what you need is to be born into the right family? But how many of us can choose our parents? But then we are back to luck.

Do we just need to get lucky to be successful?

This gets many people to become cynical and feel that the game is rigged. That no matter what they do, everything is against them.

The real question is, can you rig the game in *your* favor? Can you make it so that the odds are actually stacked for you and not against you?

Here is the Big Secret

The book, *Positioning: the Battle for Your Mind,* came out in 1981 and I bought it as soon as I saw it in the Wall Street Journal. I read it from cover to cover three times within the first week. At the time I was working for my father, which was not what I wanted. But as I absorbed the book, I realized that what I was reading could be applied to a person and that person could be me. I did not have to continue on the path I was on. My first pivot.

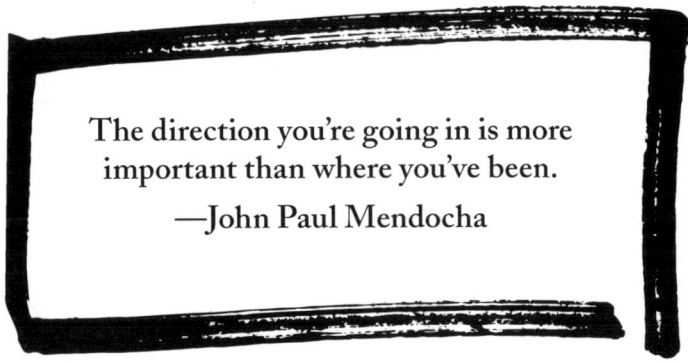

The direction you're going in is more important than where you've been.
—John Paul Mendocha

Using positioning is also not only about me going from working for my father to becoming a millionaire and also losing millions only to regain them. This is a process and a concept that is used by everyone from Elon Musk to Michael Jordan and anyone else who has been successful.

Positioning is a concept that has been with us since time began. I embraced and added layers through my work as a turnaround consultant for over twenty-six years. A system that I have honed and structured for the age of the Internet with the help of my co-conspirator, Gabe Bautista, co-author of this book.

How did this positioning concept, that was originally used by marketers and advertisers, slip seductively into our way of thinking and speaking? If positioning is as well understood as it seems to be, well then why are there so many failures? Product failures, service failures, concept failures are all around us. It seems that failure is the natural state.

Give Me a Bigger Hammer
I'll Make this Round Peg Fit

All those failures can be attributed to one factor, and that is they had inappropriately or incorrectly occupied a position that was a loser from the start. Just about anyone who has any level of ambition or success will toss positioning around—I'm going to look at what my position is going to be.

Positioning is a very subtle but powerful concept. It is all about how you rate, sift, sort and prioritize. Call it a bias because it is the position that exists in someone's head. It means that you can utilize this perception and really harness its power. The purpose of this book is to grab the concept of positioning, put it at the forefront of your mind, and teach you precisely how you can improve your situation and get to the best position you possibly can.

Do that, and success will be much more likely to take place. Stay with us, as we go through how to make sure that you are on the winning side and not the losing side, for positioning will lead the way.

Position yourself as a winner!

John Paul Mendocha
Gabriel Bautista
July, 2019
Planet Earth

For bonus materials go to:
PositionToWinBook.com

Notes

Chapter 1

Grandma, That's Not Chicken Noodle Soup

The whole thing is, you've got to make them
care about somebody.
—Frank Capra, film director (1897 - 1991)

We are what we repeatedly do.
Excellence then is not an act, but a habit.
—Aristotle, Greek philosopher (384 BC - 322 BC)

Everything has beauty but not everyone sees it.
—Confucius, Chinese philosopher (551 BC - 479 BC)

Inside of every person there is a bias map and that bias map determines what is correct or incorrect, acceptable or unacceptable. This process happens 'a priori', meaning before anything else. Before any analysis or conscious thought has taken place.

The human mind has been sifting and sorting things, putting them into categories and laying them out since time began. If your mind didn't categorize things and prioritize them, how would you know what to do?

Throughout history we have tested and tried things, we have eaten everything under the sun. Some plants killed our brother-in-law or neighbor and some vegetation didn't.

All Roads Lead to Positioning —Even The Lower East Side of New York

Before I knew what positioning was I experienced it when I was five years old and rode to New York City with my father, mother, cousin Linda and brother Michael.

To get to New York City from Denver, Colorado, in 1963 was quite a task in and of itself. It's tough when you don't have an interstate highway system, and it's even harder when you are just a kid and you're stuck in the back of a 1959 Plymouth Fury. So here is the brief travel that it took to get to New York City. If you Google it, it's 1,777 miles, given today's modern roads. We probably drove more miles than that given we went the wrong way a few times.

My father, who was a tool and die maker, had worked all day long, about eight hours, instead of his normal nine. He came home, ate dinner, took a shower, because my mother insisted, loaded up the vehicle, put my mother, my brother and I and my cousin Linda in the car, and away we went. He didn't stop until we got to St. Joseph, Missouri, 678 miles away. My father didn't believe in bathroom breaks.

The next day, we got up after sleeping whatever amount we did, which wasn't much, and took off and made it to somewhere in Ohio, and finished our journey on the third day. All I can tell you is we kids were whining, crying and extremely tired, yet my father is the guy who should have been tired since he did all the driving. My mother didn't drive.

My brother and I had filled the foot wells of the backseat of this massive car, or large to us car, with comic books and slept on top of our precious cargo. This was in the days before seat belts. At our destination I experienced the first positioning lesson that I would get in my life.

I wouldn't attempt the trip today, even without kids, given all the modern conveniences we have and how spoiled I am. It's just so much easier to fly. But I can tell you that it was a journey that I'll never forget. And it was going from one universe to another because when we arrived in New York and met my grandma, she lived in another world. It was the lower east side in a tenement building on the third floor. Wow. Up three flights. My father carried me most of the way. We barely had four steps into our house in Denver. But all I can say is that it was a Herculean task for my father to get me there, and I don't think I ever thanked him. My first lesson in positioning would now begin.

The Soup Controversy

This visit was when I met my grandma Mendocha for the first and only time. She looked at my brother and me, and asked in broken English, "Do you boys like Chicken Noodle Soup?"

My brother and I looked at each other and said, " Yea, that sounds good."

In our minds, chicken noodle soup comes in a red and white can and it says Campbell's on it. You open it up and if you want it a little richer you put less water. If you want it thinner you put a little more water and you heat it up and that is chicken noodle soup.

Grandma walked over to the kitchen and proceeded to clink, rattle and bang pots, pans, utensils and crock-ware. We heard water running but nothing productive seemed to be happening. Michael and I sat impatiently, wiggling back and forth, wondering what was taking her so long.

We discussed the preparation of chicken noodle soup in whispered tones. How long does it take to open a can, pour the contents in a saucepan, put in water, mix it up, heat up the soup, and in ten minutes it is done? You pour it in a bowl, you have it with some bread or crackers and that's it. Lunch!

Instead this process went on for what seemed like an eternity to a 5-year-old. There were lots of adults talking and walking about, different languages, elaborate gestures, discussing world events or how much milk, coffee and bread cost at the local corner store. Then, what seemed like two hours later, grandma called us over to the kitchen table.

She dished the soup into bowls and I looked down and to my horror floating in the broth was a foot. There are also other parts of a chicken that I have never seen before. Something that involved part of a neck and maybe a heart. They don't put those in a can of Campbell's chicken noodle soup!

20

Chapter 1: Grandma, That's Not Chicken Noodle Soup

My brother and I just looked at each other, Michael looked a little green. Neither of us picked up our spoon. Grandma says, "What is wrong with you boys? Why will you not eat my good chicken noodle soup? That's real chicken noodle soup!"

To which we answered her, "No", in the infinite wisdom of five and ten-year-old kids. "Chicken noodle soup comes in a red and white can that says Campbell's and you open it up and you put it in a pot and you heat it up."

Grandma scoffed, "That's not chicken noodle soup, that is garbage."

Needless to say, we were at an impasse. That was my first close encounter with a Bias Map.

Little did I know that I also got my first positioning lesson from the school of hard knocks. It would be eighteen years later, in 1981, before the value of the lesson I learned on the lower east side in a tenement apartment in New York City in 1963, came into focus.

In my mind the red and white can was right and grandma's version of chicken noodle soup with the chicken foot was just wrong.

When my father found out that his mother had been dissed, he sat us both down and said, "You have to eat the soup."

My brother and I looked at each other and realized it was going to be a very long time visiting with grandma. I moved the foot to the side of the bowl, hoping it would cling. Unfortunately it kept spiraling and spinning. That's an exercise in fluid dynamics. But that's another book.

She did end up cooking a lot of other things we liked, but, our map, our positioning of the chicken noodle soup in our brains, was simply—that isn't chicken noodle soup.

The question you should ask yourself is, whatever it is that you are doing, is it chicken noodle soup to the person that you are trying to convince of your position, or not?

> **It's all in their heads.**
> **Do they perceive it?**
> **Do they see it?**
> **Do they believe it?**
> **—John Paul Mendocha**

Summary

- Everyone has a chicken soup moment.
- Positioning is all around us, whether we acknowledge it or not.
- I didn't eat the floating foot.

Chapter 2

Why Position to Win?

Winners have simply formed the habit
of doing things losers don't like to do.
—Albert E. N. Gray, author

Don't write with sales or money in mind—
it poisons the well at its source. If winning
isn't a joy, don't do it. Life is short. Death is long.
—William Wharton, American author (1925 - 2008)

Everything comes to he who hustles while he waits.
—Thomas Edison, American inventor, businessman
(1847 - 1931)

Position to Win System is for those who realize that in business and in life we are here to win, there is no middle ground, you must win.

Anything else besides that is to lose. It is binary. You get one hundred percent or zero percent.

When there are five players in a market or five people competing for a poker pot, you might think they all have a twenty percent chance of winning, but that is not true. You have one winner and four losers. You never get twenty percent of a promotion or twenty percent of a customer or twenty percent of the pot.

Position to Win Begins

The book was born when I and my co-conspirator, Gabe Bautista, huddled in hot, humid Dallas, Texas for a day of brainstorming and planning with projects we were working on for clients. A perfect environment for an idea to be born. Gabe challenged me to show him positioning in action. We had been talking about the idea for months and how it is a central concept that I use with my clients and in the business turnarounds that I have executed.

John Paul and Gabe birth Position to Win at
Tommy Bahama's, March 2018

I had recommended to Gabe the book, *Positioning: The Battle For Your Mind*, by Al Ries and Jack Trout and he was one of the few who actually read it, studied it and got back with me to ask, "What about this? What about that?"

I had coached Gabe into understanding and using positioning in a market where he was working with a client who was trying to break into the very competitive dietary supplements niche.

Then we turned to the concept of Bias Maps and about how the human mind structures perceptions and ideas in hierarchies. Gabe once again challenged me to a demonstration on the spot of how that worked. So many theories, so few straightforward examples. Luckily, the world is filled with examples.

The Sugar Packets Bias Maps

At the time we were at a fancy Starbucks in Plano, Texas. Yes, there are actually fancier Starbucks out there called Starbucks Reserve. In order to explain Bias Maps to Gabe, I grabbed the first thing available to me: the sweetener packets tray.

Sugar Bias Map

Gabe is a Millennial, so thankfully he memorialized our afternoon of working together in his "Stories" on Snapchat and Instagram. This is a picture of that bias map.

Then I asked Gabe a series of questions to find out his own bias map, and I used the different sweeteners that we had in front of us at the time. I placed them in the order according to his preference: raw sugar, white sugar, Splenda, Equal and Sweet'N Low.

Then we talked about how a concept like this might be applied to a hyper competitive market, such as in the case of Gabe's client.

The conversation grew and grew as Gabe identified all of these concepts as related to positioning but never really spelled out in the book. He said something like, " Hey, John, I read the book but what you are saying isn't in the book."

> **The answer to any problem pre-exists.**
> **We need to ask the right question**
> **to reveal the answer.**
> **—Jonas Salk**

Spark the Fire...

Right then and there I began the journey of taking all of these concepts of Positioning, Adoption Curve, Marketing Postures, Green Field, Layer Cake, and Inciting Incident and integrating them into a Sales Funnel (or sales process if you are pre-Internet literate). Then giving birth to a cohesive program of market analysis and discovery, which I had been perfecting and using for decades, and it became evident that this book needed to be written. This book is the first Ace.

Gabe has been instrumental in not only pulling out of my head all of these thirty-seven years of experiences and concepts I have come up with along the way, but also helping to structure and blend them with his digital expertise to show how all of this can be used in the age of the Internet for an even greater effect.

Facebook Fracker Horizontally Drills Cranium of John Paul Mendocha and Cracks Details About Position to Win

Gabe demanded that I produce slides to cover the topics for the *Position to Win System* webinars. For the first one I went over the top, and out of my brain exploded dozens and dozens of pages. With very little trimming, we delivered that webinar in a little under three hours.

Evil scientist, Tom Meloche, bailed on it at about the 1 hour and 45 minute mark. Chalk that one up to small bladder. We also received our only nasty-gram from one of the beta members. "Guys, get your act together. How many slides can you possibly show me?" Something about his eyes were bleeding, his hands were numb from writing, and his ass was sore.

Gabe said maybe we should figure out how many slides we can deliver in some reasonable amount of time to get the information out. Here's a bonus for all of you—if you attempt to limit and edit the slides while you're writing the webinar, you'll end up with a big steaming pile of crap.

So here's what we did. I took my usual approach of going waaaay over the top with the number of slides. Then I thought about the slides we had. Gabe and I edited and reviewed them before I presented them. Reviewing before presenting was a new concept to me. And then, any slides that we could not get done in our pre-determined alloted time, we put behind the "The End" slide, and we called it "The Parking Lot." This made sense to me, because I'd seen Moe Howard of the Three Stooges in an interview in the 1970's describe how they did their movies. They had a basic premise that they worked from, and at some given time, when they had enough minutes of film in the can to fulfill their strict contractual agreement with Paramount, the director would yell, "Enough!" at which time all three of the Stooges would jump up and down and run around in a circle, yelling and screaming. Then they would play the music, put up The End, and roll credits. Call it Stooge Couture.

Moe applying the proper positioning

So I applied this procedure when we reached the appropriate number of minutes. We did our equivalent of running around, yelling and screaming, adding the music, putting up The End sign, and rolling credits.

It turns out that often we had more slides in the Parking Lot than in the main session. But that's in another book or books.

Position to Win System has been in gestation for many years, but now is the time for it to be released from my head into the world and for it to be widely available.

It is our sincere hope that you discover positioning everywhere and use it to your advantage. Then if appropriate, you join us in the *Position to Win System* or at any of our live events.

Summary

- *Position to Win System* brings thirty-seven years of consulting experience in the realm of Positioning and Business Turnaround together with the Digital world of the Internet and Social Media.

- Bias Maps are how people break down the infinite amount of facts into categories that they can sift and sort to make a decision or take an action.

- For more information on the Position to Win online system go to: PositionToWinBook.com.

———————— ◆ ————————

Notes

Chapter 3

History of Positioning

Great things are not done by impulse, but by a series of small things brought together.
—Vincent van Gogh, Dutch post-impressionist painter
(1853 - 1890)

Do not seek to follow in the footsteps of the wise; seek what they sought.
—Baslo, Japanese poet (1644 - 1694)

History knows no resting places and no plateaus.
—Henry Kissinger, US (German-born) diplomat
and scholar (1923 -)

As I studied the book, *Positioning: The Battle For Your Mind*, I thought it was the most amazing book I had ever read on business because it explained the various issues and aspects of why products have worked or haven't worked, and why companies fail or succeed.

31

Positioning, the concept, didn't start in 1981, however, or with Al Ries and Jack Trout, although they are known as the Positioning Guys. Their story is a great positioning lesson in itself. They acquired that position by writing their book.

Another famous advertising man named David Ogilvy, one of the brightest men in advertising in the 20th century, wrote an ad titled, "How to Create Advertising that Sells", for all media available at that time: magazines, newspapers, TV and radio. It described a list of 38 things that Ogilvy and Mather had learned about advertising and then applied to create results.

To show how deep the roots of positioning are, David Ogilvy, in his famous ad, listed positioning as number one. His few words emphasized the significance of the concept. Barely larger than a tweet, it was a delectable morsel that left the reader wanting to know more. In all likelihood, that sly fox, David Ogilvy, was teasing you to contact them to find out how to utilize positioning for your situation.

How should you position your product, service, idea or concept?

Number 1. The most important decision. We have learned that the effect of your advertising on your sales depends more on this decision than on any other: How should you position your product?

—David Ogilvy

How to create advertising that sells

by David Ogilvy

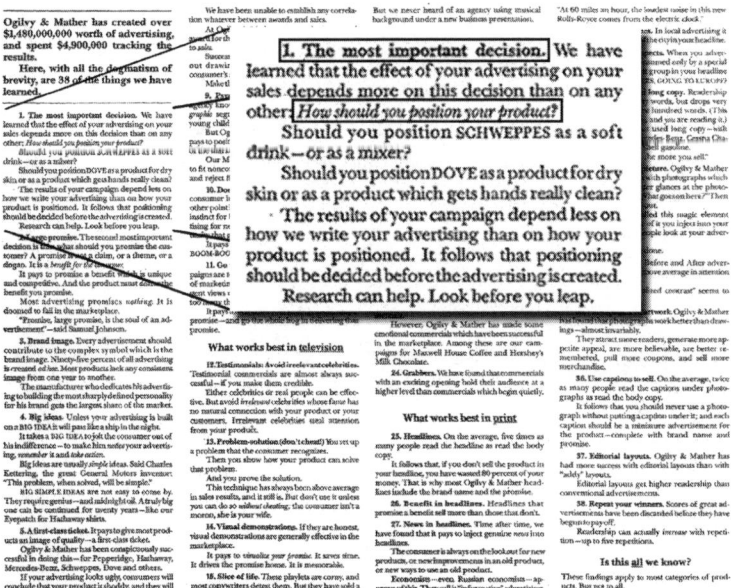

Go to PositionToWinBook.com/freestuff
to read this article in its entirety and get more free info.

Ogilvy and Mather had created over $1.48 billion worth of advertising up until the point that this ad ran. The exact dates that this ran are lost to history. Since then, countless billions of ads have been placed.

Ogilvy further states that the results of your campaign depend less on how you write your advertising than how your product is positioned. It follows that positioning should be decided before the advertising is created. Research can help. Look before you leap.

This confirms that positioning is the cornerstone of every decision that you're going to make. If you're going to sell a product, a service, an idea, or a concept, and you're going to advocate it out in the market, positioning is the cornerstone. It is the starting place to sell successfully. As Ogilvy said, it is the most important decision, and we fully concur.

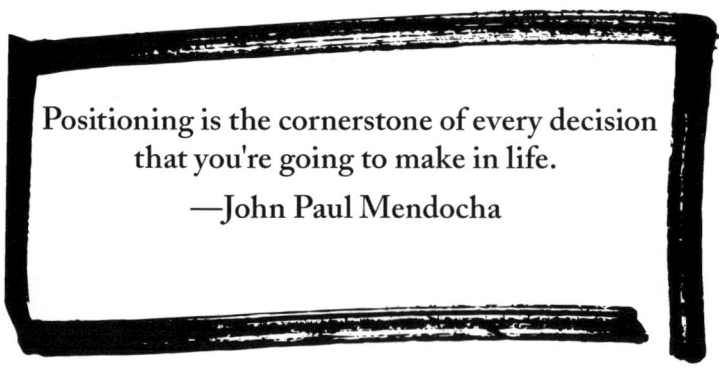

Positioning is the cornerstone of every decision that you're going to make in life.

—John Paul Mendocha

American Motors Rambler

Look at the American Motors ad for the 1967 Rambler American 220 and notice that in the ad they use the word positioned twice to describe where they fit in relation to the other guys.

"We <u>positioned</u> our compact line in the gap between the little foreign imports and the over $2000 U.S. compacts."

"A company that has <u>positioned</u> its compact Ramber American line so that 1,000,000 additional buyers can now get an automobile that's not above their means or below their needs."

They use the word positioned in the ad way back in the 60's. And even though most people don't remember the car today, at the time it became the third most purchased car in America by clearly defining where they fit.

The basic approach of positioning is not to create something new and different, but to manipulate what's already up there in the mind, to retie the connections that already exist.

August 1967 Ad LIFE Magazine

To read this ad in its entirety, go to:
PositionToWinBook.com/FreeStuff

Positioning is About Them, Not About You And That is The Key Point

Positioning is crucial and makes sense because the positioning that matters in a market exists in the mind of the receiver of the message not in the mind of the sender of the message.

Anyone who is trying to advocate a position or sales presentation usually thinks of where they are coming from and not what information the receiver is gaining. However, it should always be about what the receiver thinks and should work in the context of what the receiver already knows about you, your competitors and the rest of the market.

Your message is not received in a vacuum! It crashes upon the various bias maps that exist in everyone's mind.

> **The beginning of wisdom is to call things by their right names.**
> —**Chinese Proverb**

People are already totally committed to whatever it is they were already doing before you came along. When they receive your message they sift, sort and categorize what you say. They will then decide if you are correct or incorrect. Their mind is jammed full of bias maps always asking the question, "Is this chicken noodle soup or not?"

Whatever they come up with, for them, their decision is exactly correct: the truth to them. Trying to change people's minds is a sure way to fail and the waste of a whole lot of money and time.

Have you ever met someone from a foreign country, say, France, who does *not* believe that France is a great country? There are more patriotic and less patriotic people but they will usually have their own loyalty to their own country. They also have their own biases about where they live and bias about the religion they adhere to. These beliefs would hardly be changed by someone who comes along and says something different.

Each person has their own biases, their own level of subjectivity and limited objectivity. It is very difficult to change a mind once it has been made up. Rather you must work within that bias map for your message to have a level of acceptance.

Whenever there is a company that proclaims, "We are number one," but if they aren't number one, then the market has a tendency to punish them for it.

If four companies in a market all say, "We are number one," or "We are the best," the person who is looking at and evaluating those statements will realize that one player is correct and the other ones are lying about their position; they are counterfeit or inauthentic.

A position is something *given* to you, not something you can create out of thin air.

A bag, bucket or barrel of positioning is not available at ye olde marketing store.

The market bestows upon you a position—you can either accept it and reinforce it, or perish. The benefit of learning about positioning is that it reveals the process of sorting, categorizing and selection in the human mind.

The bastardization of the word positioning is evident in just about every marketing brochure or business plan that one looks at these days. It has become a throwaway phrase that means little.

Most do not understand what positioning is, while they use words and expressions such as, "We are positioning ourselves differently." And they usually fail miserably because they don't even understand where they fit in relation to the other players in the market and wouldn't even know where to start to find out.

The proof is in the way they behave and the message they send out into their market. They claim nonfactual status, a hyped fantasy or pure mythology and contradict their own position. Most of the time they work against their position instead of exploiting it. If you are inauthentic, the market will destroy you.

Others believe positioning is an outdated concept or one that has lost its significance. They fail to perceive that positioning has never been more important than it is right now.

Positions are not set in concrete, you have to be smart, creative and cunning to exploit your position.

Summary

- *Positioning: the Battle for your Mind* came out in 1981 but the concept of positioning is as old as the human mind.

- Positioning is all about context. It implies that you fit somewhere in the context of other players and the current marketplace.

- To hear more about positioning, case studies, stories and more, go to PositionToWinBook.com and subscribe to our podcast.

Notes

Chapter 4

Give me Positioning
or Give me Death!

Dig the well before you're thirsty.
—Chinese Proverb

It's like driving a car at night. You never see farther than your headlights, but you can make the whole trip that way.
—E.L. Dottorow, American novelist (1931-2015)

Success is simple. First, we decide what we want specifically; and second, you decide if you are willing to pay the price to make it happen, and then pay that price.
—Bunker Hunt, American oil company exec. (1926-2014)

The truth is, the more choices, the more proliferation of options, the more important positioning becomes. Most general markets are becoming more and more fragmented, with niches, sub-niches, mini-niches, micro-niches, nano-niches, pico-niches and itty-bitty-niches popping up everywhere.

From Top to Bottom Marketing

General Market	Know where you live in the food chain.
Market Segments	
Niches	This helps explain why some ideas, no matter how powerful, are destined to be only niche players.
Sub-Niches	
Mini-Niches	
Micro-Niches	
Nano-Niches	Don't kid your-self—all products, services or ideas have only so many slots.
Pico-Niches	
Itty-Bitty-Niches	

In 2018, some of the itty-bitty-niches for automobiles consisted of the following: Ferrari sold roughly 9,000 cars. Lamborghini had sales of 5,750 and McLaren Cars, 4,806.

By contrast, Porsche in the mini-niche market, sold 256,255, but most were 4-wheel drive and SUV's. The Porsche 911 sold 35,573 cars.

Lastly, the Corvette sold 9,686 cars globally, slowly sinking into the itty-bitty-niche.

How has the Corvette, an American automobile icon that has been around since 1953, sunk into its present niche? For generations it has served as a halo car for the Chevrolet division of General Motors. Originally conceived as a sports car that would appeal to American tastes—boys drooled over them and middle-aged men bought them. Therefore, it captured a part of the market that was at that point held by foreign companies. It distinguished itself by being a hot, fast, quick car: unique and different—fiberglass, the future.

The stuff that dreams are made of

Other than the first few years, it has been V-8 all the way. And Corvette is a perfect example of positioning. Over many decades, Corvette has gone through several body styles and iterations. Successes and failures. Things that had to be modified or completely changed. The 1963 Stingray split window coupe was a very unique design that ended up becoming a collectors item.

Most importantly is that Corvette stood for American speed. Decidedly aimed at that male audience that said, "I've got to own that hot car." In 1979, at its peak, Corvette sold 53,807 cars. Over the ensuing years, there has been a slow decline; it's status eroding away.

I jokingly say that Corvette was invented because of the midlife crisis. When men turn 50 or 55, they go out and buy a Corvette. It happens all the time. But things have changed. The Great Recession depleted I-want-to-play funds. And even though the Corvette is substantially better than it was years ago, it has been in steady decline. Sales in 2014 were 34,839 cars, but in 2018, it could muster only 18,791. This was the lowest production since 1959. Out of 330 million people, 18,791, cars is not that many.

Corvette is a case study in how positioning changes over time. The car is significantly better, faster, and more capable than ever. It does many of those things that one of the original, more show-than-go cars aspired to but couldn't achieve. It's interesting to watch its slow decline. Part of it is the changing ideas about car ownership in general, and also the number of options that exist. Performance today is cheaper than it's ever been in inflation-adjusted dollars.

So is the Corvette dead? Is it going to go away? The interesting thing about niches is that they expand and contract over time. The mistake that people make is they think they can create something that is like a Corvette and capture the Corvette audience; if we could just try something a little bit different but still name it a Corvette. They designed a 4-door Corvette, and a Corvette station wagon. Were they successful? Have you ever seen one on the road? This is a mistake.

So will Corvette survive? I think it will. The point is will it ever get back up to those 1979 numbers? Will it ever blow the pants off of people? Will money fly out of pockets again? And frankly, are people really interested in spending that amount of money for that kind of car? We'll have to see if the sharing economy affects this end of the market. Clearly, some of these exotics have gone up in sales volume. But still, Corvette, at the numbers they are today, sell substantially more cars than some of the rarest of exotics. For bang-for-your-buck, I don't think it can really be beaten when you look at it from an objective standpoint.

As Yogi Berra said, "If the people don't want to come out to the ballpark, nobody's going to stop them."

If people don't come to the Corvette, there's no way to make them. Because remember, positioning is all about people saying I want it, I want it now, and I have to have it.

New Chevy Corvette C-8

During the writing of this book, as part of a greater grand conspiracy, possibly from Area 51, Chevrolet introduced the mid-engine C8 Corvette, which forced us to rewrite this section. The forces of evil were obviously swirling, as all good prognosticators will tell you, highlight your exactitude, blur your inaccuracies, and deny all the rest.

The C-8 is a radical departure from all the previous Corvettes. The YouTube vloggers are ecstatic about it's potential and opportunity. Chevrolet is spending heavily to promote this fastest, bestest Corvette ever. What could go wrong?

First, will be the quality of the vehicle. Second, my father always said to never buy a car in it's first year of production. Third, is that if it is as fast and hot and value priced as it is, surely long-suffering, parched Chevrolet dealers will tack on obscene markups traveling back to a middle age time when raping and pillaging was considered a vocation.

We shall see if it moves the needle and saves Corvette. Will they ever get back to their previous status and volume? Success is not measured in fan-boy accolades, but in hard, cold cash. Will they meet the positioning challenge and take the checkered flag to success?

A Little Town in Bavaria

After the war, BMW made some of the ugliest little cars you can imagine. The BMW Isetta is a perfect example. But the boys in Munich knew that they needed something significantly better if they were going to survive in this world. Off to America they go.

Humble beginnings . . . Is there an M version?

In a classic re-branding, repositioning biblical denial that BMW ever made anything as hideous as the Isetta, they, through hard work and interesting cars like the BMW model 2002, christened themselves as The Ultimate Driving Machine. They became successful, so successful that they started to rival their big brother of Germany, Mercedes-Benz. While Mercedes was viewed as conservative and stodgy, BMW was focusing on being hip and cool. Like every great success story, BMW decided that they could sell more cars if they expanded what they offered, and they were stricken with the disease of AND.

They try to have every body style possible; for the BMW 3 series they had a car, a coupe, a convertible and a station wagon. This is dilution by AND. I will offer this AND this AND this. This is bad positioning. I don't know how profitable that is. My guess is that it confuses people, and a confused mind always says, "No." It is far better to position another vehicle next to it and name it something completely different.

BMW 3 Series

Funky, Quirky and Defensible

Subaru is an example of a company that drilled down into a niche, found a winning strategy and a loyal following.

They created a defensible niche. It was an odd ugly duckling car with looks that only a mother could love.

Subaru positioned itself as a car that delivered a 4-wheel drive for adverse conditions. It wasn't designed to go off-road like a Jeep. It was an economy car that could be driven down a highway in just about any kind of weather, and deliver the security of a 4-wheel drive.

Subaru has been formidable in holding onto their niche and defending off anyone.

In the 80's, Toyota flirted with its own version of a 4-wheel drive with the Tercel. In fact I owned one for years. But when I tried to replace it with a new Tercel with the 4-wheel drive, I discovered that that option was not available. I would have to buy a Subaru.

Now the Subaru sacrifices potential buyers outside of inclement weather states, but they proudly hold onto their niche today.

Breaking out of a niche is also tough, but a company can survive and prosper in its own comfortable, defensible niche.

Every Market is Dynamic

Positioning is simple, but what is increasingly complex is the way in which markets are breaking down into smaller pieces: down to the individual, the 7.6 billion biases, the individual likes and dislikes.

While we do have many shared values which drive biases, in the end we can only convince and persuade those whose mind is compatible or receptive with our position, or else adapt our message to those presuppositions. Every mind is a vault door and you don't have the combination, yet you need to learn how to get in.

Do You Know The Combination?

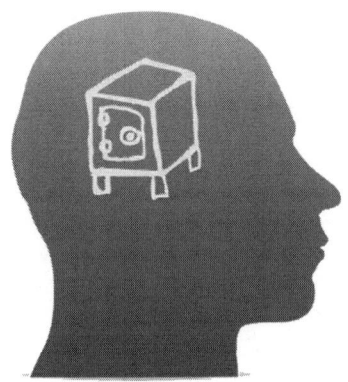

The mind is a locked vault

Every one of the prospects or customers or anyone else that you meet, essentially has a locked vault that is their mind. Now, if you know the right combination it's relatively easy to sell to them, to persuade them, to convince them that your path, your method, what you're going to do is significantly better than other ways to do things.

But how do we know the combination to that safe door or that vault door?

It comes down to understanding that everyone has biases—lots of different kinds of biases. And each of these biases affect how people will make a decision. Some people like steak, other people like chicken, others are vegans. All of them are correct in their own minds. There are those who are coffee drinkers. There are those who get up every morning and drink a Coca-Cola. There are many who drink tea and there are still others will have some other green, pink or blue concoction. All of these various biases make up what goes on inside their minds.

The vault has many different combinations. Knowing exactly what the combinations are for that specific person you're trying to influence, or group that you're trying to encourage to change their way of thinking, is the key to the *Position to Win System*.

It is finding those series of combinations that open up the most doors with the least effort. Have you ever tried to convince somebody of your ideas and your methods just to find out that they never seem to agree with you on anything?

Now, they may call themselves a contrarian or they may say that they just have a different point of view, or they're giving you the devil's advocate position. But all of that resistance means one thing, you don't have the combination.

Getting Behind the Vault Door Doesn't Guarantee There Are Riches for You Within

Now, it doesn't necessarily mean that if you had the combination to their brain that what you're offering matches up, because once you open up their minds and you find out what that combination is, then you're faced with the realization that sometimes what you're selling doesn't match what they're buying. It doesn't fit to the combination that's inside their head.

A great example of this kind of situation is the Qwerty vs Dvorak keyboard. The guy who invented Dvorak, created a more efficient, much faster, less hand-stress keyboard. Dvorak unlocked the vault door for people who wanted a better experience. But so far, no one has said they're going to teach Dvorak instead of Qwerty. A classic case of building a better mousetrap and then finding out that the mice are lactose intolerant. He set out to solve a problem, he solved it, and nobody cared.

Make no mistake, customers who don't fit your situation can still be valuable. A joint venture perhaps, but that's more of an advanced concept and a different way to think.

Every single mind is already predisposed to say, we want this very specific series of things in this kind of order and once we see them, we say, "Of course, that fits."

Have you ever had the experience of saying, "Wow, I just found your company, product, service. I wish I had known about this years before. Where have you been?"

To which you smile and say, "We've been here all along. All of the years you've been searching, we've been looking for you. We never found you. You just found us. It all came together. There you go."

Opening up that mind vault is so critical and that is one of the reasons why the *Position to Win System* was developed.

Values Drive Biases

I traveled to Disneyland with my niece, Patti, and while there I carried around my American Express tote bag. She commented about how nice it must be to be rich. I was a little surprised, given the way I was dressed. Patti pointed at the tote bag. "What?" I asked.

She remarked, "Well, you have an American Express tote bag, which means you must have an American Express card. And that is only given to people with money."

In her mind having an American Express card meant a certain level of affluence and status. That was her value based bias. In my mind, it was how much money I bled through American Express, and all they gave me was a lousy tote bag!

Each of us was being driven by our values observing the same tote bag. Whatever is taken for granted, assumed and is familiar is a reflection of your values. Your values drive your biases.

How Big Is Your World?

I was in Denver visiting with my mother, when a roving nurse came to visit. Nurse Nancy says to me, "Your mother tells me that you travel quite extensively."

"Yes, for business."

"Oh, that must be very exciting. You must meet so many interesting people and see such exotic places."

By this stage in my life I had been on so many flights that I viewed an airline as a bus without the class.

Nancy is waiting for me to tell her about all of my exciting travels. My mother is smiling happily, waiting for my insights to be imparted to Nancy. I didn't want to disappoint either one, so I asked the nurse if she had ever taken a flight. She was in her mid thirties, and grew up in rural Colorado. "I don't have any family that I need to fly to see. Everyone I know is within driving distance."

For Nancy the thought of flying was a romantic allure. For me being crammed in a metal tube, flying at 37,000 feet—the heart flaming mystery of such an event had long since died.

Not wanting to burst her idyllic bubble, I encouraged Nancy to map out a trip and take a journey to a distant land. My suggestion was San Diego and the world famous zoo. That would be a great place for her to go.

The more that you assume that everyone has the same values, and, therefore, will have the same biases, the more difficult it is to obtain a viewing point to see what your position truly is compared to theirs.

Limited Experiences, Limited Scope

My wife, Rebecca, and I were at our Lawrence Welk timeshare by Escondido, California and we had just seen *Menopause: the Musical* at the Welk theatre.

We were talking to a lovely couple who sat next to us, and after the show we continued the conversation. They lived in Sun City West in Arizona, and loved the area except for one caveat. The wife said there were really no good restaurants in Sun City West, so they had to go outside for the good restaurants. "Our favorite Italian restaurant is Olive Garden and we go quite often," she said.

That short, brief statement spoke volumes about positions on Italian restaurants.

Not all pasta is created equal

There is nothing wrong with Olive Garden. It's just that our favorite Italian restaurant is Il Mulino in The Forum Shops at Caesars Palace in Las Vegas. According to urban legend, the New York location is considered one of the best Italian restaurants in mid-town Manhattan, often frequented by many dark suited, dark tie kinda guys. They have a tendency to be very particular about what kinds of Italian food they partake of. I have yet to see one of them in any Olive Garden I have ever eaten at in my entire life.

From Wine to Whiner

I was doing a turnaround for a client and was traveling with Bill, a member of the staff. Concerned that I wouldn't know what to do with my evening, he suggested I go to dinner with him, his wife's sister and her husband.

He made it sound like I was in some barren, inhospitable land, unable to fend for myself. The city was San Francisco.

I said I would be OK, having traveled all over the world by myself, I think I can handle an evening by myself in the city.

He persisted.

I acquiesced and we were off to meet his relatives.

Of course, we went to a seafood restaurant. Small talk ensued and Bill's brother-in-law, a large man with an ill-fitting shirt, asked about my wine preference for each of the courses.

I explained to him that I had been sober since January 2, 1986 (but who's counting). If I had hit him with a baseball bat at close range, it would have had less impact on his oversized cranium.

"What? You don't drink wine? Jesus drank wine."

"Jesus had twelve disciples so he could have had his own twelve-step program."

I thought by this time he would get the hint, but he persisted, pointing out that the French drink wine starting in the 5th grade. Though he did give ground by pointing out that they dilute children's wine with water.

I asked him if they used Perrier.

At this point the wine dude showed up with his little silver tastevin cup on a chain that you could tow a Ford F-150 with.

The sommelier clasped both of his hands around brother-in-law's hand and vigorously shook it. "Welcome back."

Clearly they had a relationship.

Chapter 4: Give Me Positioning or Give Me Death

He asked what wine we were going to start with and pain-in-the-ass looked at me derisively and quipped, "Some of us aren't drinking wine tonight."

The wine dude saw tip money fly out of his outstretched hand. However, in an effort to broker a détente, he pointed out that they had an extensive beer and cocktail menu that met everyone's taste, and that as hard as it was to believe there were some who did not understand the virtues of the grape, he would be happy to bring me something else. He jokingly pointed out that this was San Francisco and one had to keep an open mind.

They finally reached a break in their discourse and I remarked that I would be having water and decaf coffee. My level of pissed-off-ness drove me to tell the sommelier that I was going to have (gasp) tap water.

"That just can't be done, sir." He offered me five different types of bottled water, if I could just be reasonable. Since the brother-in-law was paying I selected the most expensive.

"Excellent choice."

At that point the brother-in-law quipped, "My life's goal is to build my wine collection to 2000 bottles."

"Is your wine cellar earthquake proof?" I questioned.

He frowned, "That thought keeps me up at night."

"Maybe you should be tapping more of those bottles to help you sleep." I surmised.

Disturbed that his universe had a distinct out of balance wobble, he dug into the fifty page wine menu for solace, muttering that it was going to be a difficult evening selecting wine for only three drinkers.

Clearly this is a man driven by his values and biases and everyone he knows is as obsessed as he is with wine. Those with similar values believe that their version of the world is absolutely correct and not only that, they also typically hang out with each other.

We All Are Fighting To Be Heard Over the Noise

You are fighting to get clients' attention and their time, while all of your competitors are vying for the same. Every person believes that they are correct and that everyone else lives in a world of hypocrisy.

Positioning matters because if you want to be heard, if you want to be believed, if you want to convince, if you want customers to bend to your direction, you have to position yourself properly or they will not listen to you at all.

It is time to take charge of your own positioning and not let it happen to you at random, which is what usually happens. This is a bad thing. But if you take charge and really think things through, you will have a vision of the market or the terrain that no one else has.

Knowing the shape of the terrain gives you the home court advantage, which has several aspects that are often overlooked and underutilized. Sun Tzu recognized this 2500 years ago.

This insight provides valuable advantage as you apply the principles of the *Position to Win System*.

> The natural formation of the country is the soldier's best ally; but a power of estimating the adversary, of controlling the forces of victory, and of shrewdly calculating difficulties, dangers, and distances, constitutes the test of a great general. He who knows these things, and in fighting puts his knowledge into practice, will win his battles. He who knows them not, nor practices them, will surely be defeated.
> —Sun Tzu, *The Art of War. Book X. Terrain*

How Favorable or Hostile are the Odds

Would you play a Roulette wheel with one hundred slots instead of the customary thirty-eight slots with thirty-six numbers plus 0 and 00, with the same odds? It would be a terrible money losing proposition. Positioning is stacking the odds in your favor and then and only then, coming to the table to play.

Can you position yourself in a way in which those who you're are trying to persuade will listen to you favorably? They will either react positively, negatively or they will be ambivalent or neutral. The people who you want to continue to engage with are the people who are reacting positively to your position and are sympathetic to it.

Without careful consideration and strategic thought you will become the cork bobbing up and down in the ocean while you are hoping to get to some destination but in all likelihood you are not going to get very far, which is why we know:

Most Businesses Fail in the First 5 Minutes. It Just Takes them 3 to 5 Years to Realize It

This book is dedicated to those who do not want to fail in the next three to five years. Those who want to go from the darkness and move towards the light, to position themselves and not be destroyed by the market, but win the market.

Without it, you are building on no foundation at all.

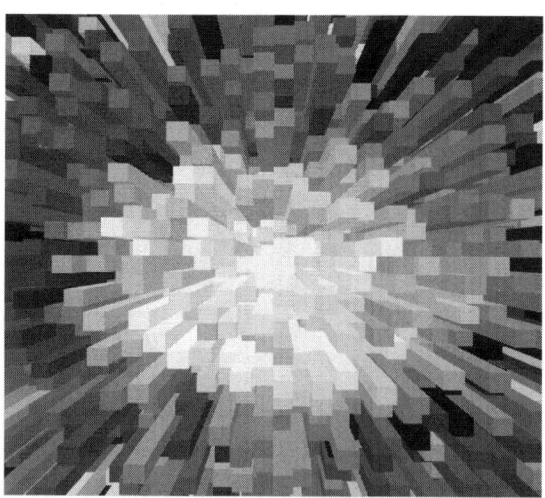

Everything was going along just fine and then The Big Bang happened...

Summary

- Ever fracturing markets and multiplicity of choice makes the concept of positioning more vital than ever. If you don't want to get lost in a sea of options you *must* understand and exploit your own position.

- The *Position to Win System* takes a rational, reality broad view of the market. Without careful analysis and thought you will fall into the category of being something for everyone and eventually be found out to be nothing for all.

- Understanding positioning means not only that you know where you are and how you fit but also where the other players are and the shape of the entire terrain. Learn from Sun Tzu and know your terrain or perish.

- Most businesses fail in the first 5 minutes. It just takes them 3 to 5 years to realize it.

Notes

Chapter 5
Positioning Traps: Barriers to Success

If you want something you've never had, you have to do something you've never done!
—Kimnesha Benns

Our mind is like a parachute. It only works when it is open
—Anonymous

A pro is someone who can do great work when he doesn't feel like it.
—Alstair Cooke, British-born American writer
(1908 - 2004)

The road to success is neither straight nor smooth, but filled with twists and turns, roadblocks, impediments and challenges. So now let's talk about the barriers that people encounter time and time again when trying to position themselves, their company, product, service or idea and some thoughts on how we can avoid these Positioning Traps.

1. Not Having Staked Out a Defined Position

We have a tendency to accept where we are and say things like, "This is our lot in life," or "This is who I am," when in fact we are the ones who decide what position we will stake out. Do we go one way or another way?

What are all of our choices that define the position that we have? The mistake that people make is that they believe that this is some random event.

Your position is only random when you don't take control of it and "just let it happen," whether it is your job or the reception of your product in the market. Know where you are, know where the other people are, and then you can make a decision and actually be proactive in regard to your position. You can test different angles and maybe go deeper into your own position or pivot.

Take control of your own position and stake out a defined one. Only by doing it consciously and deliberately will you be able to position yourself to win.

2. Not Acknowledging Those Who Are Already There

Very few people will be able to say that they are totally "unique." Mark Twain is attributed to saying: "Adam was the only who could honestly say, 'I said it first.'"

To which I would add, and Eve interrupted and said, "No, you didn't. Don't you remember? I told you that a week ago."

Part of positioning is recognizing the wider context, which includes the other players or competitors who are already there. If you do not take into account those who are already there and believe that your decisions or those of the market are made in the vacuum of space, then you are setting yourself up for failure before you even begin.

3. Not Understanding the Difference Between Being Unique and Being a Commodity

As difficult as it is to accept, being unique requires you to be different. Everyone, of course, loves to be unique, but no one really wants to be different. You can't eat your cake and have it, too.

Being unique means you cannot be all things to all people. When someone calls you at your business and tells you they want to give you feedback that is contrary to the unique position that you hold in the marketplace, they will never be a customer. Do not fear them—their feedback is irrelevant.

Insecurity drives many business owners to misinterpret feedback and mistake the marginal (outlier) customer from the true customer. Being unique means that you apply the rule of the Sharp Edge.

A commodity is a raw (primary) material. It offers little to distinguish itself from the other offerings in the market. Therefore, its value is reduced to the lowest common denominator.

When viewed from a distance there is a tendency to start thinking of everything as a commodity. Many want to categorize subjects or people into three primary colors (raw materials), with no unique attributes. However, the three primary colors can create a vast amount of color combinations beyond primary; there is a pallet of 16.7 million colors available on a computer monitor beyond the white, black and grey.

The realization or fear that you are falling into being a commodity means that you have accepted the restrictions and that you have given up control in defining yourself in a different way.

If you are defined as a commodity in the market, you are no longer in control of your position and your advantage. When you devolve into a commodity, you are on the downward slope.

Coffee is a commodity. Starbucks turned it into something other than a commodity by repositioning themselves from the lowest, cheapest loss leader offered by restaurants to a luxury item that people went out of their way to enjoy. It was not coffee as an afterthought. It became a coffee experience.

We will constantly fight throughout our entire life, career and business with being grouped with others. The reason why that happens is that every person you encounter sifts, sorts and defines where you fit according to their frame of reference, or bias map.

It's the path of least resistance. There is no way out of that trap; they see you how they see you. The question is, do you reinforce that perception or do you provide evidence to the contrary?

Everyone's Favorite Station

Hard to believe that 100 years ago millions of people would sit in front of a wooden box and carefully tune their radio to bring the world into their home. When, in fact, since the beginning of time, that person, every person, everyone, is tuned to precisely one frequency—the call letters are, WIIFM—What's In it for Me?

Now I know some syrupy altruist is screaming at the book saying that's not me; I listen to other people. We are hardwired to hear, simply, what's in it for me. This is at the core of every bias map, the hub, if you will, that each bias map spawns from. It is unchanging.

We look at our smart phone, grumbling that the latest YouTube video is running a little slow and the resolution isn't perfect. This is a manifestation of WIIFM. You don't need to be an astronomer to know that the center of the universe, on this planet, is harbored in the minds of 7.6 billion (and counting) inhabitants.

Visualize a four-year-old at a birthday party and his mother says you can have any color balloon you want. Excitedly he races back to where the clown is standing next to the giant helium tank—hopefully he isn't huffing any—as the clown asks in his high pitched voice, "What color do you want?"

The boy just watched little Sally walk away with a red balloon. He says excitedly, "A red balloon."

The big red-nosed clown with the huge shoes and orange, pink, blue and purple hair shakes his head and says, "Sorry, she took the last red balloon."

The child goes from ecstatic to particle accelerator meltdown. The clown shrugs his shoulders, "It's ok, there are lots of other pretty colors."

But the boy had in his head, a giant, 500,000 watt transmitter blasting that he's not getting a red balloon.

Even though it's in your head, WIIFM is loud and clear—each person hears their own version. This is not something that has to be taught. Disappointment and expectations usually do not match up to reality.

Mix Your Colors into a Rich Palette

Like the primary colors you might have one or two things that you do. You might be a lawyer or a plumber or you might sell technology or real estate or you might sell a generic product or service that a lot of other people sell. How will you blend and mix those primary colors? What will your recipe be? How will you create your own unique shade to really stand out? And once you do, will you have the bravado to bare the label of different when you become truly unique?

Values are a suite of biases. Think of a hotel and a lavish suite. Maybe a penthouse. All the rooms if strung together are filled with biases: family, religion, education, comedy.

Jeff Foxworthy has made a pretty comfortable living with his redneck humor. Larry, the Cable Guy, delights millions with his portrayal of a cable installer.

Comedy works only because we have shared biases which tie into stereotypes. You can only make fun of somebody and their behavior because mannerisms and speech patterns are stereotypical and contrast with other behavior.

With pure political correctness there can be no comedy. No contrast. No comedy.

Denying Reality is Never a Good Idea

Trying to eliminate all biases flies in the face of mother nature. To try to use wisdom and knowledge to not have our perceptions drive us is counterproductive. Our perceptions drive us.

Tail of the One-Eyed Cat

We had a one-eyed cat named Leila. She lost her eye early on as a kitten because before it opened, it was destroyed by a virus. She was forever-after treated as a pariah by her mother, by her sisters—even Blackie, the house dog shied away from her.

Even though they had known her for years—she was different. The biases the animals had explains why everybody wants to be unique but nobody wants to be different. To be different means to be an outlier. To be an outlier means you don't fit comfortably into the herd.

Most members of a herd blend, but not with the environment, they blend with each other, like the zebra. Being black and white does not help you to blend with the grass, but it helps you to blend with the herd if every other zebra is also black and white (or white and black). The safety then, is in the herd. Like zebras, people gravitate to the herd.

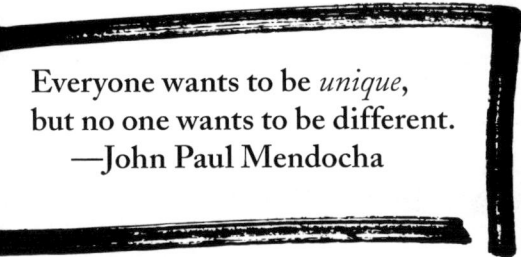

Everyone wants to be *unique*,
but no one wants to be different.
—John Paul Mendocha

4. Lack of Clarity

Now you have to deal with the limitations of the market you are in.

Humans are faced with a myriad of choices every single day, whether it was a thousand years ago and of course even more so today, we are faced with the challenge of what to do right now.

Today with the availability of technology we have access to more choices than ever, though these choices don't necessarily mean that we are going to be more successful, more capable, happier or satisfied.

This myriad of choices might make it harder to be successful because we are overwhelmed by the quantity.

When you look up how many different SKU's Amazon sells, as of June 2019, you get all kinds of different answers from different so called "data" companies. Amazon does not publish this information. The figures range from a low of 21 million to over 606 million SKUs world wide.

Regardless of what the true figure is, the point is clear: they sell a lot of different products, virtually an infinite amount of choices.

If you only spent 1 second looking at 606 million products it would take you over 19 years to view them all without stopping to eat or sleep. This presents a tyranny of choice that confuses the mind. Simply put, a confused mind always says, "No."

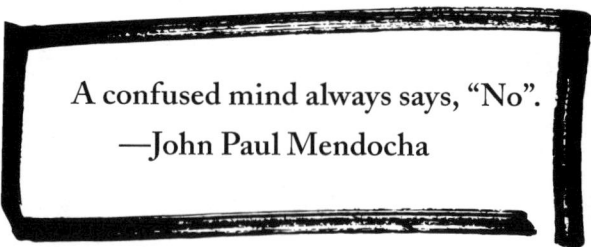

A confused mind always says, "No".
—John Paul Mendocha

And while Amazon sells a myriad of things it doesn't mean that *you* should. Amazon didn't start out by selling everything, they started just with books. Such initial focus propelled them; you should focus also.

If you keep adding things to your position you will lose focus and confuse people. The best example is Starbucks—they sell coffee.

Every time they have tried to sell other things, like CD's, they have lost money. It is amazing that it took them as long as it did for them to close Teavana which they were going to package to sell to tea drinkers. But it turns out that tea drinkers are not the same as coffee drinkers.

5. The Rule of AND

Whenever you are trying to place a position out in the marketplace, whatever that market happens to be, the more you say "and" as in, "We do this AND this AND this," the less clarity you have.

This reminds me of a yogurt place that my wife, Rebecca, and I used to go to all the time. We loved it. It was a great treat. We liked it so much we had to be careful not to go too often or have to loosen the belts. It was that good.

The guy who ran the place really understood how to present a super great yogurt experience. He hired young, attractive coeds who never ate the yogurt.

He then decides to sell the business and the new owners come in and they are going to make it better. They get a bright idea about how to fix it. They are going to drive it to the next level.

What do they do? They decide to add something else.

Every time you add something to an on-going concern you create a divisor.

Originally, when you walked into this frozen yogurt shop you became intoxicated, almost euphoric, by the sweet sugary smell. The cool, crisp air added anticipation of a mouthful of smooth, creamy delight.

To our dismay, the new owners made our skin crawl like nails on a chalkboard. For their AND they put in—

Hot Dogs!

Greasy, Smelly, Hot Dogs!

The links were the first thing that you saw and smelled when you walked in. We said, "Hot dogs?" We could see them getting crispy as they whirled around and around on the spit.

"Yes", he remarked, "Being so close to the theatre, I thought they would be a great addition to the yogurt."

He even offered us a special deal on the hot dogs, which we declined. When we drove by a few months later, there was a For Lease sign and when you looked in the former yogurt shop, all of the equipment was gone.

It took them less than ninety days to kill a business that we had been frequenting for over four years.

That was a lack of clarity.

6. Denial of Your Own Position

The irony of the human condition is that the majority of people do not like who they really are. This is the problem that Marilyn Monroe ran into when she desperately wanted to be known as a great actress, and not just the pretty, sexy bombshell.

Sometimes when you become successful in life the very thing that is the breakthrough success, that very success that you have been so desiring to happen, in your mind, seems like your worst attribute.

Marilyn was obviously attractive, alluring, had cha-
risma, men wanted to do all kinds of things to and with
her. Hugh Hefner would say that Marilyn single handedly
launched Playboy magazine; the lust factor was incredible.

Marilyn would say to her friends and to everyone who
would listen that, to her, that was the worst thing, this
voluptuous body, this incredible sexiness that ultimately
kept her from what she really wanted to be—recognized as
a great actress.

Marilyn Monroe in the film Niagara, 1953

That is denial of a position that she occupied in the
minds of millions of people. The position she denied gave
her power, money and success.

Another example of denial of position was the rock
band Warrant, who was in the process of releasing their
second album that they were going to call *Uncle Tom's Cab-
in*. Don Ienner, the president of Columbia Music wanted a
rock album song similar to "Love in the Elevator" to finish
out the album, and they needed to have it fast to

meet their deadline. Under that pressure, lead singer, Jani Lane, takes a pizza box, flips it over and hurriedly scribbles out a song in fifteen minutes. The song was "Cherry Pie".

Jani thinks it is such a ridiculous song that they dedicate it to Ienner as a joke. They record the song and follow it up with a music video. Bobbie Brown, a very scantily clad model was cast in the music video which made tongue-in-cheek references to provocative parental warning labels. The album gets banned in certain countries because the video is so salacious.

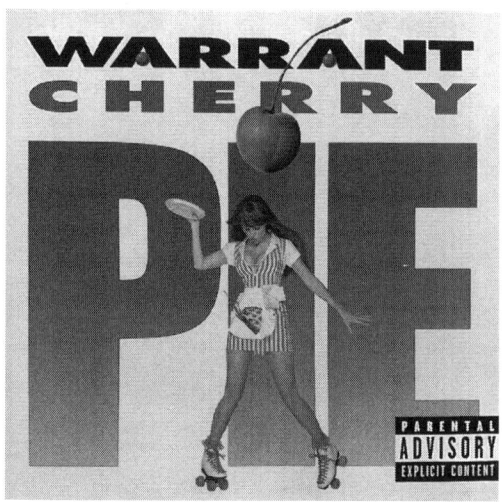

Number one selling song for Warrant

However, the song is a huge hit. The biggest hit Warrant ever had. It currently has 42 million views on YouTube and counting. The pizza box is put on display at the Hard Rock cafe in Destin, Florida.

Warrant goes from guys who are trying to figure out their position, to guys who make a ton of money and were invited everywhere. Wherever they play, people want to hear "Cherry Pie." Jani is incensed.

He eventually moves to a Malibu beach house, and even marries Bobbie Brown, the hot model from the video. But for the rest of his life, sadly he died young, he says he hates "Cherry Pie." He says it is a slap in the face of his musical capability and the worst thing that could ever happen to him. This is an example of denying your own position.

This happens to people over and over again. Instead of exploiting their talents that have made them successful, they want to do something else. This is a significant deterrent to long term success.

7. Undervaluing What You Already Have

We live in a world where we can see and hear and think about the endless possibilities of life. This creates an immense sadness and belief that we are lacking something.

We don't know if there is such a thing as a "lack" gene. Some people are just cursed with this genetic defect. But you see this over and over again when people say, "If I only had this or that," or "If I only had what other people have."

When I gambled professionally, poker taught me one thing. You have to play the hand that is in front of you. If you don't, then you are frozen, unable to act, to adapt. Not to mention that you are burning valuable time.

You Have to Play the Hand That is in Front of You

Undervaluing what you already have means that you will search for the silver lining instead of dealing with what you have right in front of you. Oftentimes that means giving up the success that could have been.

Domino's Pizza

Domino's was started in 1960 when brothers Tom and James Monaghan put down $75.00, and borrowed $900 to buy a pizza store named Dominick's in Ypsilanti, Michigan.

The next year James wanted out because he was unhappy with the speed by which the pizza parlor was taking off. So Tom traded his brother a used, beat-up 1959 Volkswagen Beetle the brothers had used as a delivery vehicle, in exchange for his 50% share in the business. The brother drove off quietly into the sunset.

Today Domino's Pizza rakes in more than $10 billion annually. In 1998 Tom Monaghan sold his controlling stake in the company to Bain Capital, an investment firm based in Boston, for an estimated $1 billion.

Talk about someone who undervalued what he already had. Hopefully that Volkswagen is still running—you never know.

Summary

Positioning Traps: Barriers to Success

- Not having staked out a defined position.
- Not acknowledging all those who are already in the marketplace.
- Not understanding the difference between being unique and being a commodity.
- Lack of clarity.
- The rule of AND.
- Denial of your own position.
- Undervaluing what you already have.

Notes

Chapter 6

The Power to Compel
Success or Failure

*The temptation to form premature theories upon insufficient
data is the bane of our profession.*
—Sherlock Holmes (Sir Arthur Conan Doyle, 1859-1930)
The Valley of Fear

*Many of life's failures are people who did not realize how close
they were to success when they gave up.*
—Thomas A. Edison, American inventor, businessman
(1847 - 1931)

*Far better it is to dare mighty things, to win glorious
triumphs even though checkered by failure, than to rank with
those poor spirits who neither enjoy nor suffer much because
they live in the gray twilight that knows
neither victory nor defeat.*
—Theodore Roosevelt, 26th President
of the United States (1858 - 1919)

Most Businesses Fail in the First 5 Minutes
It Just Takes Them 3 to 5 Years to Realize It

The "Aha" of this book is the stark realization that most businesses fail by aiming at something that ultimately they cannot hit, because it violates the rules of positioning. Having said that, it is not only that they fail, or that they fail within the first five years. Rather, in our experience, these businesses make **fundamental mistakes in the first five minutes** that lead to their sad, grueling and slow eventual failure—but only after all the energy, capital, credit lines and investments are exhausted.

The reason why they fail, and this is almost always true, is that they miss one of the seven key Aces that we outline in the *Position to Win System*. They incorrectly position themselves.

It does not mean that you are guaranteed success if you read this book. What it does mean is that if you actually apply these positioning steps, you will probably not get into many of the businesses, markets or business models that people start, only to find out that it is not going to work.

It doesn't take a rocket scientist to figure out that mixing hot dogs and frozen yogurt is not a good idea. Even if they were sincerely trying to improve their business. Talk about lack of self-awareness! But you would be surprised to see how many people make mistakes of positioning in their business, albeit more subtle ones.

How could the yogurt guy have solved his problem? By following these steps:

> Know your Position
>
> Accept your Position
>
> Have a Message and Position Match

Hopefully you will realize that your business could fail in the first five minutes and you won't accept it for three to five years after you have spent considerable time, money and resources. Many people do this and come to the conclusion that no one can be successful.

Nothing can be further from the truth. If you are aware and apply the seven steps of the *Position to Win System*, your business will have a much greater chance to be successful.

The Human Folly and Tragedy of the Challenge

From a very young age we look up to those who have conquered the unconquerable. We idolize the comeback. We talk about David vs. Goliath and all the while we are suckered into the folly and tragedy of the challenge. You never hear about David's full fight record. Sure he beat Goliath, but what about others he beat? Is he the odds-on favorite you would be betting on?

This mistaken belief has cost countless millions to lose their shirts in business. Why? Because they have cool posters that tell them they should endure to insure success. All without understanding that raw determination is not close to being a success formula. It is far better to find a game that you can win at and become the best at. The danger of spiraling up aspirations is that the universe is only too ready to kick your ass.

Who hasn't experienced having a seemingly great idea that is completely out of reach? Literature is no help. We all love the story of *Moby Dick* and Ahab fighting against all the odds, or *The Old Man and the Sea*. Though it may seem dramatic and virtuous, it will put you into a position of weakness.

Winning by betting on a long shot makes for great bar room talk. Hoping that a miracle will pull it out for you is a mistake that you shouldn't pursue. Make sure that you find that game, market, product, service or idea that works for you. Exploiting that to the best of your talents is by far the best way to succeed in this hyper-competitive world.

When you look at your competition, always think in terms of how you can exploit your position to overcome any resistance to your success. There is no additional pay-off, other than an ego stroke, by constantly fighting against the headwinds of superior competition.

I have experienced many companies that did not accept their position in the marketplace and sought an unreachable, unobtainable position only to crash and burn. Sadly, it appears that this is a fault not of logic but of the human psyche.

Deal Yourself a Winning Hand

Most people have never had a chance to think in those terms. They have never come to the realization that you don't have to live with the cards you have been dealt. You can deal yourself a winning hand: Aces and not 3's.

When you look at the statistics of business success you discover that over fifty percent of businesses fail after five years. Depending on the class and industry it can be upwards of eighty percent and if you look at a period of ten years it can be over ninety-five percent of businesses failing.

The reality, however, is that they actually failed in the first five minutes and they went through a long period of agonizing painful, slow death eating away at their own capital or investment. Borrowing here and borrowing there, hoping against hope that they might hit a breakthrough in the process, not only wasting capital and resources but burning valuable time.

Summary

- Most people can draw a correct conclusion when faced with some data to analyze. The problem is usually in the initial assumptions that are made in the first five minutes. If those assumptions are not true, it won't matter how much money, time or resources you throw at the problem. It will not succeed.

- The *Position to Win System* walks you through seven specific steps of analysis, thought and finally action so you understand what your upside and risk potential really are.

- No one has enough time to make all of the mistakes they need to make in order to learn to be successful. Find a shortcut. Positioning to win is that shortcut.

- Put yourself in a favorable position and tilt the odds in your favor.

- Deal yourself a winning hand.

Notes

Chapter 7
Misconception About Positioning

Misunderstanding is generally simpler than true understanding, and hence has more potential for popularity.
—Raheel Farooq, Pakistani writer and teacher (1986 -)

"Honey," the wife says,
"Is it ok if we take the luggage on our trip?"
Husband: "No, it's airplane luggage and we're taking the bus."
—Old Vaudeville joke

Language is the source of misunderstandings.
Antoine de Saint-Exupery, French writer (1900 - 1944)

The largest misconception that I've run into about the concept of positioning is that it is only about advertising. It happened to me when I first read the Ries and Trout book in 1981. I handed the book to my father, a very fast reader.

He read through it, and said, "John, interesting, maybe. Doesn't apply to us. We don't advertise. It's a book about advertising."

Talk about letting the air out of the balloon.

That was my first encounter of a negative kind that boxes up positioning. It happened less than a week after getting my hands on what would become the most profound book in my life. The idea that positioning is only about advertising is a misconception, because positioning is all about the bias maps that exist in everybody's head.

Close Encounters of a Bias Kind

Once you start to understand that bias exists all around us, it becomes easier to understand why we are correct and the rest of the world's wrong. Our bias maps tell us what we believe is true—undoubtedly we must be right.

Then we meet somebody and they seem to be making sense, but they are speaking a foreign language, not a real foreign language, but a bias map foreign language. We say up, they say down. We say left, they say right—tomato, tomahto, potato, potahto.

There is a significant amount of polarization. If you are in the middle of a civil conversation, they'll say a polite thing: "I guess we just have to agree to disagree." Which is a nice way of saying, "I think you're full of shit."

It means you've run into somebody's hard bias map that this is the way the world should work. It also explains the divide between different groups, generations, cultures, and any variety of disciplines. These biases drive us to seek out— especially in today's digital world—confirmation, validation, and rationalization of our positions. There are many out there who will accommodate you. It is hard to accept the simple statement that perception is reality.

We have a bias map about everything. The reality is that everybody you meet—your spouse, your significant other, your kids, their school mates, your peers at work, the industry that you're in, your boss, your employees, customers, prospects, everybody—has their own bias maps and their own sense of the rightness in the world and the way it works.

Whiskey Talk Is Cheap

We fast forward and now I'm doing turnaround consulting and I've run into the classic Mr. #1 CEO in a restaurant bar. He spoke very boldly about the company's position in the marketplace. He could beat any foe and best any competitor. His goal was simple—in the market he was in, they were going to be #1, even though they were number none. He'd made up little laminated cards that told everyone this. He rallied the troops. Part of hiring me was to make this happen. His words were direct and simple, "You're the hot shot. You're the one who can make this happen. Let's go kick some ass."

What came to light was that instead of being in the top two or three in this marketplace, they were one of the mutts. His brain was stuck on the obsession that if we just think positively, and work hard at it, be diligent, that we're going to magically become the top dog. A codicil in the law of positioning is that this kind of inane thinking never gets rewarded.

He decides we are going after a project worth $5 million dollars in the first round. It represents a 35% increase in gross sales. I explained that this is going to be a difficult, arduous task. A *Lord of the Rings* level pain in the ass. He poo-pooed that. "Let's go out and make it happen."

I point out that in order to win a $5 million dollar deal, a substantial investment will have to be made to chase after this opportunity. I tell him that he should expect to spend between $250,000 to $300,000 dollars. The CEO reacts very negatively telling me that I am just looking for excuses.

So I jump into the fray against seven competitors. And with a budget of less than $50,000, we start chasing this massive opportunity. Two vendors are eliminated, now the competition is down to five, and we have made the cut.

Then the customer eliminates two more, and we are in the final three. Each successive round that we survive, the CEO chides me that I was being over-dramatic when I said we needed at least $250,000 to win the opportunity. A miracle happened, and we made it to the final two. Then a funny thing happens. The customer whose opportunity we are chasing says, "Well boys, now it's time to get serious."

We fly to meet with them and they tell us that we now need to spend real money to make it to the final and maybe win.

If you haven't guessed by now, Mr. Make-it-Happen-Let's-Think-Positive, punked out. The trophy got awarded to the Big Dog. In a case of self-delusion, not wanting to spend more money, the CEO sat there and whined, "I'm going to take my bat and ball and go home."

Fast forward almost twenty years later. The company I did the turnaround for is out of business and the Big Dog is bigger than ever. That opportunity still exists and has paid many million of dollars to the winner. It's a great idea to use guts and luck to stay alive in the game, but remember that the winners are positioned in such a way that they win again and again. People who are ill-positioned are very brave in the bar with a whiskey glow, but when the CEO had to put the money on the table, he didn't do it.

That is, in essence, what positioning is about: the order in which you place things, how you think, what you believe. Everything is laid out on your bias maps. Now, one could call it preferences. They could say, well, I prefer this over this. If you want to see a great example of that, go to any restaurant, and you'll find out that your idea of what is the best meal that you could get is not what somebody else believes. And whenever you have this belief that everybody thinks like you do, well, in fact, they don't. When other people project their own beliefs on you, their own biases, their preferences, you either find common ground, which is agreement, or you find disagreement. It is usually a mixture of both.

> **Common ground is an agreement of bias maps.**
> **—John Paul Mendocha**

Positioning is all about understanding that this exists. It will continue to exist. It will always exist. Because that is how human nature works. We break down, we sift, we sort, we categorize, we pull things together, from the youngest of age, to the oldest. We always are saying what is good or bad, right or wrong. What we believe is true. All of us continuously believe that this is exactly the best, or the correct way to think. All the other beliefs are wrong. We are the ones who are right.

Advertising, being this very unique form of communications in humans, means that we always have to deal with positioning. Advertising is the crucible where every communications method has to be tested. If it can survive in that hot oven, that annealing severe trial that burns off all of the impurities about any idea or concept; if it can survive in that advertising space, then it can survive in any other human interaction. No, positioning isn't just about advertising. It's about communicating in the most profound and significant way.

87

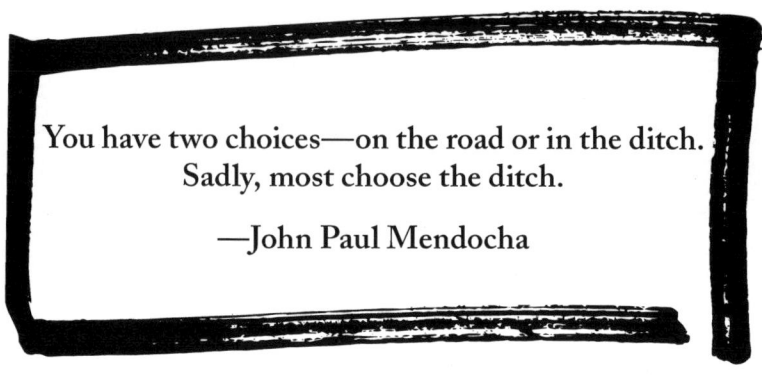

You have two choices—on the road or in the ditch.
Sadly, most choose the ditch.

—John Paul Mendocha

Summary

- Positioning is the fundamental, the cornerstone, the first decision you must know and understand. Positioning is so important that it has become an expression that everyone uses—but it has lost its meaning and gotten confused and misunderstood.

- While positioning is widely used in the advertising world, positioning is much more than that. It not only applies to advertising and how to position a product or a business, it is the mental process of organizing information and therefore its concepts apply to any category of information stored in the mind.

- Positioning is an ever existing principle that will outlast any technological change and fad of the week. Use it well and you will be ready to take full advantage of any opportunities that arise.

Chapter 8
Message to Position Match

The medium is the message.
—Marshall McLuhan, Canadian philosopher from
Understanding Media (1911 - 1980)

*All of us failed to match our dreams of perfection. So I rate us
on the basis of our splendid failure to do the impossible.*
—William Faulkner, American author and
Nobel Prize laureate (1897 - 1962)

Since we cannot match it let us take our revenge by abusing it.
—Michel de Montaigne, philosopher of the French
Renaissance (1533 - 1592)

Once you have a position and you know it, and understand it, you hit this hard rock wall. Whatever your position
is, defines what you can and cannot say and do.

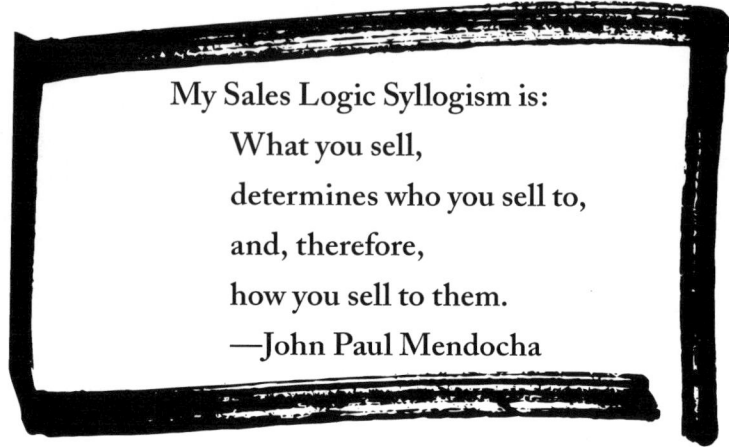

My Sales Logic Syllogism is:

What you sell,

determines who you sell to,

and, therefore,

how you sell to them.

—John Paul Mendocha

Converting prospects to customers to clients requires that you know specifically how and why they buy. Which brings us to why message to position match is extremely important.

Your Position Always Comes First, Your Message Second

Your message cannot be authentic if it does not mirror your position. A bald headed barber creates concern for the middle-aged man. The market made up of individual buyers determines what is true, authentic and acceptable in their minds.

Many experts believe that it doesn't really matter as long as you are selling to people. I quit drinking that Kool-Aid about twenty years ago.

If Starbucks came out with a smart phone, someone might buy it if it actually was able to make an espresso or a Frappuccino® or something frothy, but that would probably be the extent of its market share. People who want a smart phone that can make coffee—probably not the biggest market.

Stretching Beyond Credulity

Even if Apple came up with a product that was
totally out of bounds for the company and it wouldn't match
anything else in their portfolio, it would undoubtedly be a
failure. Even if it came from a super-successful company like
Apple.

Many mighty companies make this mistake countless
times. No matter how successful you are, you are bounded
by your position.

The mistake that so many people and companies that
have a well-honed and defined position make, is that they
decide that since they have this herd of people or big list of
customers then they can go out and sell them something
else or even anything else. In most cases, you can't.

It doesn't mean you can't partner with someone and
leverage your position, but your message always has to be
congruent and therefore match your position, leaving little
to no room for the competition to be heard. Fail to do this,
and you jeopardize all that you have built.

This Venn Diagram has two circles: Your Position and
Your Message.

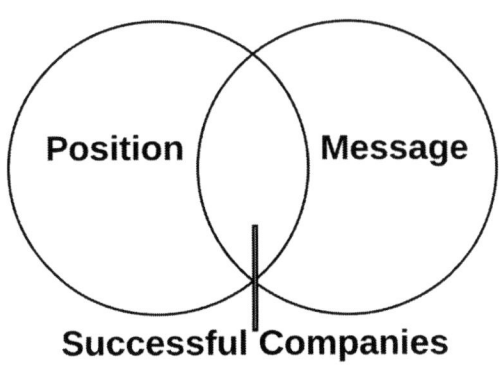

The farther apart they are, the more diffused they are, and the less effective they are. The most successful companies are the ones that make their message and position almost indistinguishable from each other.

It doesn't mean you can't go out and do something else but it is more difficult. History is filled with many examples of people who had the right position and the wrong message and others who had the wrong position and the right message. In either case, if that is you, then you won't be that successful.

Again some of these examples are from people who gained a measure of success but who never really went through a period of acceptance of where they were and why they got there.

This is Marilyn Monroe, the ditzy, blonde bombshell who says, "They love me, but I don't want to play sexy. I want to be taken seriously." She felt she was typecast—typecasting is positioning.

Marilyn Monroe helped launch *Playboy* magazine, started fights with husbands and jealous wives, and became a world-wide sensation. Ministers from the pulpit talked about the blasphemy of *The Seven Year Itch*, and her skirt blowing up when she was standing on the grate.

She then plays an absolutely serious role in *The Misfits*, an Arthur Miller film directed by John Huston starring Marilyn Monroe and Clark Gable which failed at the box office. If this film involved so many incredible people directing and acting in it, how do you mess up? You miscast the lead role.

This was a really tough acting position, and she did a great job, But if people can't see you in that position, it makes them uncomfortable and they feel uneasy—grinding of gears and gnashing of teeth. People didn't accept

Marilyn in such a serious role. They didn't accept her in that position. Total mispositioning.

Remember, positioning is always about the perception in the mind of the person who is receiving the information, not the one who is sending it.

From Stardom to Close-Outs

A less elegant example happened when I was at a store called Big Lots. They sell at extreme close-outs—that means market failures. I discovered these cans of no fat re-fried beans with a brand name that I knew. To make them, all the food processor did was to leave out the lard. They were selling at 80% off. As I wheeled my cart filled with these cans to the check-out counter, two young cashiers were speaking to each other in Spanish. They asked me in English how many cans I had.

"Twenty-four."

They continued speaking to each other, clearly refer-ring to my selection. I asked them what was wrong. They both smiled and said, "It's the lard that makes them taste so good."

I pointed out that one could buy these cans of beans and since lard is extremely inexpensive, one could put a dollop of lard in each can to get to that magical place. They looked at each other with a surprised expression; this gringo had cracked the code.

The woman who was checking me out said, "I'm going to go buy some of these cans because they are so less expen-sive."

I smiled at her and quipped, "I bought the last 24 cans."

This perception and the positioning of what constitutes the good beans prevented them from seeing the possibility of "doctoring" these beans and making them "right."

Positioning in a can.

Who Would You Place as General?

This happened to me when I watched the movie *Patton*. I thought the movie was incredibly amazing. George C. Scott won the Oscar for best actor, and the script was by Francis Ford Coppola and Edmund H. North. And because I went to the smart kids school, I just had to go to the archives and get a recording of the real George S. Patton.

George C. Scott, Faux General

To say the least, there was dissonance. There was frankly a destruction of the world around me, because in the recording, General Patton had a high, squeaky voice and didn't do a lot of great speeches.

It didn't mean that he didn't communicate well, it is just that the position that was already resonant in my head was the Academy Award winning performance that George C. Scott delivered. When the real Patton delivered the message, it made my skin crawl.

If I was going to have someone command a bunch of tanks I would have had the guy with the squeaky voice. But if I was going to have a guy portray me in a movie, I would pick George C. Scott.

This happens over and over again. Failure to pay heed to this means that your message will not match the real position out there.

George Patton, aka, Old Blood and Guts

He earned the nickname Old Blood and Guts because critics said he had a lust for battle without regard for his troops. However, the opposite is true. He produced more results with less loss of life than any other general in any army during WW II.

The World's Best Enchiladas
This is Getting it Wrong

Gabe and I ate at a nice enough restaurant for breakfast in Arrowbear, California. It had ten or twelve tables and was perched on the wide spot on the side of a mountain road with a sign that stated—The World's Best Enchiladas. That is probably a position that they cannot hold on to.

Just because you say it, doesn't make it so

The World's Finest Automobile
This is Getting it Right

Rolls-Royce has been acknowledged as the "World's Finest Automobile," for over 100+ years. Every king, queen, duke, earl, president, despot, movie star and anybody who is anybody who has had one says, "OMG I have arrived." The Rolls exudes exclusiveness and status wherever it is seen.

The danger of having a message to position mismatch is destruction, it is not tenable. Having a message to position match enhances your ability and your options, it leverages all your capabilities and everything you have put on the table. This makes it all "click." This differentiates you from others.

Slumming at $500,000

From Genes to Jeans—Who Buys What?

In the end, yes, there will always be people who will buy the cheaper, and the cheapest. One could walk into a Walmart, which I have done when I needed to buy something cheap, and buy a pair of jeans for $9.99 that are of a certain quality and they have a position and a message.

But you probably won't find a pair of Lucky brand jeans that sell for $340 at a Walmart because they probably would not sell many of them.

However, if you do wander around in downtown San Diego in the tony Gaslamp district where they do sell Lucky brand jeans, you will see all these people walking in buying jeans for several hundred dollars. If you showed up and saw Walmart style jeans, then my guess is that the tried and true customers of the Lucky brand would probably never come back again.

This sharp contrast between the two is the reason why you must be aware that you have a message and you also have a position and those two must match and if they don't match you're out of luck.

The Metric System

Best Western Hotel in Milan, Italy

Best Western hotel in Milan. Yes, Best Western. Why would anyone pay the franchise fee to put a Best Western hotel in Milan? I didn't know but Giorgio told me.

Chapter 8: Message to Position Match

We found the Best Western hotel during a Car Guy tour through Italy. All the guys in the group have a lot of money. Ed, for example, has a concrete turntable in an underground garage where he parks his seven Ferraris. When he has a party, people can come and look at his exotic car while it slowly rotates and they can feel bad about their own car or life just as slowly as it turns.

While staying at the Best Western I meet Giorgio, the manager, and I ask him, "Why in the world are you guys the Best Western hotel in Milan?"

And he says, "Well, it is simple. When Americans come to Italy and see us, they recognize us. If we were the:

Palazzo Matteotti

Sina De La Ville

degli Arcimboldi

Residenza Porta Volta

Isola Libera

people would think, what do those letters mean? They would not even come in. But when we have the Best Western sign and you are from America, even though you have never stayed at a Best Western hotel before you say, "Oh I know what that is."

By the way, all the signage and everything else at the hotel looks like you were in Iowa. I asked him what kind of people they get at the hotel and he said, "We get Americans and Germans. Italians don't stay here or French or any other European people. Just Americans and Germans."

There is a big giant sign that says they are AAA rated, and what the American Automotive Association is doing in Milan, I don't know, but the big sign says that they are a Five-Star hotel.

We all go to our rooms, jet-lagged, and when we come back down to the lobby, here comes Ed, the guy with the seven Ferraris and the concrete turntable. He has this crazed look in his eyes. Ed lives in Bel Air, California and so has a lot of first-world problems.

Ed says, "Hey, I wanna know something? How in the *hell* is this a Five-Star hotel? I can barely get in the shower. When you use the toilet you have to put your feet in the shower because it is so small!"

Ed goes on to complain to Giorgio and keeps talking about it, while Giorgio gives him a half English, half Italian spiel which was his way of saying, "Look, I don't have an answer."

So I say, "Hey Ed, let me help you out. You see you don't understand. They have a different grading system for hotels here. It is a metric system, it is five out of one hundred. Ha!"

To which Ed says, "You are damned right about that!" and stalks off.

Giorgio says, "Hey, that was good." Because he understood the metric system joke, like if that was actually a thing. However, he was smart enough to know that the right position was to become the Best Western hotel for the people he wanted to stay at the hotel. That was the right position and the right message.

Summary

- Once you know and understand your position it is of utmost importance that you align your message with what your true position is.

- You may experience resistance in aligning these two, especially internally and from other insiders.

- Your market though, will understand very clearly who you are and what you do. It will click for them inside their mind. On the other hand if you have a message to position mismatch you will most likely not be very successful or fail altogether.

Notes

Chapter 9

The Fine Art of Pivoting

Don't dance for the audience; dance for yourself.
—Bob Fosse, American dancer, musical theater
choreographer, theater and film director (1927 - 1987)

*To me, boxing is like a ballet, except there's no music, no
choreography, and the dancers hit each other.*
—Jack Handey, American humorist (1949 -)

*There comes a point in everyone's life that we either stay the
course or venture beyond to a new world. This is the point of
the pivot, to move our sights to the sky!*
—John Paul Mendocha, Entrepreneur and author

Are You Stuck, Stuck, Stuck?

Everyone has a position, and we have constructed this whole process so you can become aware of your own position and accept it. This doesn't mean, however, that you are stuck or that you are somehow anchored to this position.

Pivoting means you are *not* stuck inside of your current position. If you rotate a few degrees and move forward, this changes your trajectory to what could be a better vantage point.

Now does that further goal still look like what you want to do? Are you going to continue to pivot or stay on the new course you just moved to?

If you are a circus clown, and one day you wake up and decide you want to be a jet fighter pilot, that's probably not going to happen. That is a suicide mission.

If Apple decides it wants to be a food chain, would this work? No, because that is too far outside their present position. What you can't do is to change your position completely in one big leap, but you can learn to Pivot.

The IBM Pivot Story

> **Nobody ever lost their job for recommending the purchase of IBM products.**
> —Computer Industry Folk Wisdom

I became aware of the significance of IBM's continuous pivoting from Peter Drucker, who was a consultant to two titans of IBM's success, Tom Watson Senior and Tom Watson Junior.

The Computer-Tabulating-Recording Company (CTR) was founded on June 16, 1911, by the merger of three small businesses by financier Charles Ranlett Flint. Despite the progress the tabulating machine line was making, as a whole C-T-R stalled in its first years after the merger. So, in 1914 he hired Tom Watson Sr. as a general manager and it was the best decision he ever made.

In 1915, IBM made four million USD in business machine sales. By 1980 their gross sales were 26.21 billion with net earnings of 3.39 billion. IBM became so large that the United States government filed an antitrust suit against them.

Big Blue

How did IBM stay in business so long and be such a force in the market?

Over many decades, Watson focused resources on tabulating machines, which are essentially mechanical counting machines. These machines could count faster than others and be used to collect data.

Before the (C-T-R) merger, the machines had been used to conduct population censuses in a variety of countries, including Austria, Canada,

Denmark and Russia. Not only could the machines count faster, but they could understand information in new ways. In a census, for instance, a single card, about three inches by seven inches, could be punched with holes that form an information portrait of a person—city of residence, age, nationality, job and more. Hollerith's [who invented the tabulating machine] contraptions were able to sort through millions of cards and count how many teachers lived in Chicago, Illinois, or count any other subset of the population. Society could learn things it never knew it could learn, and at speeds no one thought possible.

Businesses quickly realized that the portraits on those cards didn't have to be citizens, but of a product a company sells, or a freight car on a rail line, or an insurance customer. Early adopters of the electric tabulation method included the freight office of the New York Central Railroad and the Eastman Kodak Company, which used a tabulating machine to keep track of customers and salesmen.

Internet source: IBM100 IBM is founded.

C-T-R was selling products at that time with the United Kingdom, Canada and Germany. Tom Watson continued the expansion to more countries and decided that he needed a more inclusive company, so in 1924 he renamed C-T-R, International Business Machines (IBM).

Watson focused on the global market while most others had very little international diversification.

The First Key Pivot

Tom Watson Sr. was the one who made the decision that IBM should continue in the business of being a tabulating machine company. He selected that as their *position* which they pursued quite successfully.

IBM had expanded so rapidly during WWII, that the company knew it had to make changes to deflect a potentially difficult situation by having a U.S. market slowdown. So the company *pivoted* into the international market to accelerate its growth. In 1949, to manage the foreign operations to further strengthen his international position he formed the World Trade Corporation, which would produce half its bottom line by the 1970's.

In 1951 Tom Watson Jr. is now the chief executive. His father passes away in 1956 at age 82.

The Second Key Pivot

Remington Rand introduced a Univac computer in 1951. A year later IBM introduced its own mainframe computer and many thought that the company was too slow to market and would fail. However, within five years they had 85% of the market—a dominant position.

A Univac executive complained, "It doesn't do much good to build a better mousetrap if the other guy selling mousetraps has five times as many salesmen."

In 1943, ironically, Tom Watson Sr. said, "I think there is a world market for maybe five (mainframe) computers."

How did IBM gather 85% of the market? By ingenious pivoting.

Watson Junior sees that they have to remain in the area of helping businesses with transactions and calculations. That's their solid position. The other companies in the computer business at the time were trying to do scientific and other computing.

IBM decided to do the most mundane thing with computers. They were going to focus on business transactions. What can be more boring than accounting? No scientific experiments, just balancing the books. But IBM started to work towards that in the computer space, and how did they do it? They did so by pivoting.

To solve that problem, IBM decided to think creatively about the business model itself. They would try a model where they would lease computing cycles to businesses as opposed to selling them a computer. In other words, selling them a service and not a product.

Buying a service would have been far too abstract for people to grasp, so the way they sold it, was by telling businesses that they would charge them per cycle. They would charge a little fee to help them keep track of things. They even positioned their fee as a business model.

Some might have thought that IBM was stuck and they would not be able to seize a new or different position, but by first becoming aware and accepting what their true center was—working with businesses and helping them with transactions—IBM was able to successfully pivot.

The Result? At one point IBM ends up becoming the biggest computer company in the world. In fact, all of their competitors in the mainframe business end up becoming known as the seven dwarfs. And let's face it, between Snow White and the Seven Dwarfs, it is Snow White who gets the top billing. Snow White gets to go to the beach in Cabo and the Dwarfs get to open a car dealership in Pacoima.

The Third Key Pivot

By the late 70's Watson Jr. decided to change, or pivot away from being just a mainframe computer company and work towards becoming a personal computer company. How would they go about making this pivot?

This was a new field and at the time many people didn't even understand why they needed computers. Many claimed that the total available market for computers would always be small.

In 1977, Ken Olsen of Digital Equipment said, "There is no reason anyone would want a computer in their home."

Yet IBM wanted to make that bet. But they knew they couldn't just leap from being a mainframe company to being a personal computer company.

How did they take all of their skills and their existing customer base and figure out what those customers wanted in a computer? Counter-intuitively, what they discovered is that no potential customers wanted a computer.

Most people would have become disheartened and walked away concluding that the naysayers had been right. Not IBM.

Teaming Up with Microsoft

They set up a separate group to develop the personal computer, and made a deal with Microsoft for the operating system. The unintended consequence of that pivot was to make William Gates the Third, the richest man on the planet at one time. Without IBM validating Microsoft who knows how big Microsoft would have become.

*Harvard Dropout
and Billionaire*

The PC market grows so explosively that IBM can't control it, and the personal computer and computer technology becomes ubiquitous. They reach mainstream status. Computers are no longer relegated to some far off room. Now millions of workers around the globe stare at screens everyday. Households buy them by the millions.

They proliferate rapidly through all grade levels of schools. Eventually they are everywhere. The rise of the network is coming and eventually the Internet. That combination kills all other personal computers, mini computers and word processor companies with the exception of Apple. To save a rain-forest we won't list them all here. In 2019, Bill Gates is worth 103.8 billion dollars.

IBM was able to stay in business through all the changes in the industry because Watson and those after him made correct choices and pivoted to keep themselves a flourishing company even today. Even though they lost control of the personal computer market, with massive change they were able to survive.

That cannot be said of Wang, Radio Shack, Data General and any number of other players in the market that have faded away.

One hundred and eight years after its founding IBM's 2018 revenue was 79.6 billion with net income of 8.72 billion dollars.

Steve Jobs

Now let's look at an example of an individual doing pivoting. Steve Jobs attended Reed College but doesn't really do much in the way of formal academic education. He ends up coming back to Silicon Valley while everything is exploding in the technology space and he gets a job at Atari working for Nolan Bushnell—which probably gets Steve a "get out of purgatory" card. May not have needed it, in the end, but it didn't hurt.

While working for Bushnell he meets Steve Wozniak whom he will eventually partner up with to create Apple Computer. At the time though, it seems that Jobs is the worst person Atari could have hired because he was always off in his own space, doing what he wanted and not doing his specified job.

Then Jobs realizes that to be his own man, he must pivot out of being a technical guy to being a promoter and eventually to being a business guy. So he teams with Wozniak, becomes the business guy, and starts showing people the Apple I. By the way, this model is now worth a lot of money as a collector's item.

At the time they are working out of his parents' garage and what Steve does in a short period of time is, through a series of pivots, becomes a world class presenter.

Barely attended Reed College— never graduated

Anyone who wants to see how to present product launches should watch Steve Jobs. If you could present just twenty percent of how well Steve presented, you would do well. Even young Steve, with the bow tie, to old Steve, at the end, with the turtlenecks that cost more than most people's suits, could hold a crowd in his hand to perfection. The massive changes he made in his life were all a series of improvements towards becoming that person in the mind of the crowd. In our way of thinking, a series of pivots.

> **The reality distortion field was said by Andy Hertzfeld to be Steve Jobs's ability to convince himself and others to believe almost anything with a mix of charm, charisma, bravado, hyperbole, marketing, appeasement and persistence.**
>
> **It was said to distort an audience's sense of proportion and scales of difficulties and made them believe that the task in hand was possible.**
>
> **—*Reality Distortion Field, Wikipedia***

In the computer industry all you have to say is Steve and everyone knows who you are talking about. He passed away too soon, but attained mythological status which is the ultimate positioning.

You Too Can Pivot

The beauty of positioning is that you are not stuck with where you are. What happens though, if you want to go from frozen yogurt to hot dog, you are taking a chance when you break the frame, which is like glass, that exists around your current position.

Doing pivots that your customers accept works; doing large leaps that your customers don't accept, doesn't work.

The point of doing pivoting is that even if you are an individual who has built a position, you can still change it by nudging yourself along in small hops to get where you want to go. You will then continue in that trajectory. A cumulative effect happens when you start pivoting.

John Paul's Pivoting Story

This is my own story of pivoting. When I read the book *Positioning: The Battle for Your Mind*, I realized that I didn't

want to work for my father for very long so I needed to move in a new trajectory, setting and course. Therefore I went to work for an office products company where I found out that their idea of office automation was anything that has a cord that gets plugged into a wall. Their office consisted of collators, decollators, paper shredders, typewriters, copy machines and sorters. Talk about a trivia question!

Up to my ass in . . . opportunities

From there I convinced them to start thinking about becoming a computer dealer, which they never actually did. They become my first consulting client and I computerized their business even though I didn't know how to run a computer or how to do double entry accounting. But I realized that if I could be one or two chapters ahead of them, I could make this work.

Eventually, they did purchase a computer. At the same time I was helping them by selling products and being a sales guy. While doing that, I sold more paper shredders than anyone else and realized that I needed to take advantage of more opportunities in the tech space by selling more complex technology. This became my next pivot move.

In 1982 I landed a job at Westek, a manufacturing rep company, which is the lowest form of animal in that whole supply chain. My brother, Michael, worked there even though he graduated with honors with a BSEE.

John Paul Mendocha

Westek Data Products, Inc.

To my father's chagrin, Michael became a salesperson instead of an electrical engineer.

Jim, the owner of Westek, was skeptical that I would be knowledgeable enough with the technology to be able to sell, so he made me a deal. I would have breakfast every morning with my brother and he would teach me the technical aspects of the products we were selling. I was a quick learner and got more use out of Michael's BSEE than he ever did.

Then I used positioning, the book and also the concept, to position myself as someone who did what none of the other sales people in the office took the initiative to do—computerized my leads.

Everyone in my territory was in my computer. Then I would mix in my direct response marketing background and I knew I could do things with that list that most people couldn't do.

By the way, Jim saw what I was doing and got the office manager, Kathleen, to get a computer and start punching in those leads so they could have them, too. I would have given them a good deal on my list if they would have bought it and then I could just transfer it to their computer. Oh well.

The Westek position exposed me to a broad set of technology companies that I could potentially work for. When you think about pivoting don't think that it is a one step from Zero to Hero. That is not a pivot. A pivot is a movement around a center that changes direction and trajectory. Even the slightest pivot changes the trajectory that becomes more pronounced over time.

To finish the story, Westek gets an award and while at the sales meeting I sit next to George, the VP of Sales and Marketing for Data Systems Design, one of the companies Westek represented. He was a co-founder and Stanford graduate. Some time later, my first ride in a Ferrari was in his.

George began talking about *In Search of Excellence*—he raved about the book. I told him about *Positioning: the Battle for Your Mind* and asked him if he knew about the book, and he said, "No."

"Do you know about positioning?"

George affirmed he did not. So I said, "Let me give you the Positioning Test." I give him three positioning questions. He gets them all right because they hold the dominant position in the market.

George screams out, "David, get over here!"

David, Director of Marketing, appeared quickly at the table. "David, do you know the book…" George looks at me and says, "What's the name of that book?"

"Positioning: the Battle for Your Mind."

David genuflects and blesses himself and remarks, "This is our bible for marketing."

Now George is even more intrigued because he himself has not read the book, so I tell him not to buy it, that I will FedEx a copy to him.

The Gauntlet Interview

I send it out to George and a few months later when I go to interview for Data Systems Design, I walk by George's desk and I see the book that I had FedExed him, with post-it notes and paper clips all over.

The human resources person is, of course, blown away because she doesn't understand how I have this pull with one of the co-founders of this successful company. It is quite simply because I had positioned myself differently from other sales people.

Chapter 9: The Fine Art of Pivoting

Becoming a Data Set of One

How many sales people did George meet over those number of years? How many of them bought him a book with great insights that changed what he was thinking about? I was always seen in his eyes as "The Positioning Guy" which was a powerful position.

Fast Forward

From there, that gets me to California and two jobs later I get to my signature job which makes me six figures a year and gives me enough stock to make me a millionaire, the first person in my family's lineage to ever do that.

All of that from a series of pivots which I worked at consciously. Part of looking for pivots is to ask yourself, "What is my destination?"

And if you realize you can't get there in one hop or two hops then figure out how you can keep progressing in that general direction. This way you can get closer and ever closer to your desired position.

Not bad for an investment of $5.95 for a paperback book and $21.00 for FedEx to ship it. Now that is a return on an investment.

Why is Pivoting Possible?

People will accept a modest change of who you are. When you make that change and when you hit that point where you rotate and move forward to a new position, the next time that you do the pivot and you look back you will see the distance and the point where you started. The change and angle of where you started will become significantly different and it will compound over time. It creates a cumulative effect.

> **Most people overestimate what they can do in one year and underestimate what they can do in ten.**
>
> **—Attributed to Bill Gates**

At first the pivots and hops might be small, even too small for you to notice consciously. You might have already done these types of moves and never considered that you did anything different. Like when you changed jobs or departments or moved to a different city. Now, with this awareness and insight you can go out and consciously pivot to where you want to go.

Success is the Relentless Pursuit of Moving Forward

After you go through The Five Dimensions of Personal Positioning, which we will discuss later, and you figure out how those are going to work in your life. Then you will be able to look at your talents and your capabilities and find something to do and somewhere to go that will significantly increase the position that you have. The caveat is that most people who find a place and a position, get a little too comfortable and don't necessarily figure out how to continue the process.

Death Race . . .

In the wee dark hours of the morning, there are untold multitudes training to run a marathon. For some, it's on their bucket list, for others, it's an obsession. All want to be known as having bested this grueling race. Ironically, the derivation of the name marathon, comes from a city in Greece.

In ancient times, (before Twitter), during the Battle of Marathon, the messenger Pheidippides, ancient Greek for Chuck, ran 25 miles from Marathon to Athens, to deliver the exciting victorius news that the Persians had been defeated. When he arrived, he threw up his hands, his fists tight, screaming, "We have defeated the Persians!" A cheer erupted from the populace. At that moment, he clutched a folded hand to his chest, collapsed in a sweaty heap and died instantly.

In spite of this tragedy, around the globe, hundreds of marathons are run every year, not necessarily delivering the message, but delivering the runners a winning attitude. For those who are obsessed, this is a calling. If you're going to be an entrepreneur, a successful one, get your head wrapped around the idea that you are perpetually running a marathon.

Running a Marathon Like it's a Sprint

This is the same mistake that people make when they work hard on getting a joint venture put in place. Eighty percent of the energy and effort goes into getting the deal set up and almost no energy is expended in making the venture a success.

You can start right now. Become aware that no matter where you are you can begin to pivot. Remember you can pivot sooner rather than later. This gives you a huge advantage over everyone else in your field. That's where the sweet spot is. Give yourself a goal and an expectation of where you should be while at the same time not futurize too much because there are a lot of things that are not under your control. Then you can start to pivot toward those goals and at the same time not miss opportunities along the way.

Get Your Bearings Straight
Before You Commit to a Pivot

It is the difference between true north, magnetic north and marketing north. Make sure that you are not making a mistake by going on some kind of tangent inside of your head. Rigidly thinking this is the way I want to go and this is what I want to do, while missing opportunities right in front of you.

The long forgotten tech companies that only exist in people's memories made the same mistake. Those that had a vision of what they wanted to do and where things were going to go but as markets started to change and move, they died. They did not or could not adapt and pivot towards where events were headed.

North, True North And Marketing North

They were stuck with their initial goals, visions and assumptions. And as Jesse Livermore, the famous stock trader, would say, "The market is always right."

So you too must have a level of flexibility in what you think your path is.

Can we imagine if YouTube, which started as a dating site that allowed people to post videos of themselves, did not recognize that they had an opportunity to become something else? They pivoted. (Most people don't know that.) Unfortunately, many are too stubborn or too committed to their original idea.

It is like crouching down by the edge of a river and while facing the opposite direction of the current start to yell, "Wrong way, wrong way!" If you are a Marvel Superhero you might get the river to change direction, but for the most part the river is going to continue to flow in the direction it is. The question is, how do you use the natural direction of the river to your advantage and not to your demise?

Pivoting is all about finding those advantageous turns—to change direction and trajectory ever so slightly and make small hops so you can end up in a completely different place than you started.

And, where do you want to get to? The place where you have consciously positioned yourself to win.

> **A pivot is a conscious movement which sends you on a new trajectory, setting and course.**
>
> **—John Paul Mendocha**

Summary

- When working to change your own position, and after going through the process of awareness and acceptance of your current position, think about the smallest possible pivot you can make that changes your direction and trajectory towards that new position you are seeking.

- Never try to leap to a new position—Zero to Hero is usually a formula for disaster.

- Look at the examples of IBM, Steve Jobs and John Paul Mendocha. What lessons can you draw up that can help you make pivots that continuously improve your position?

- In the beginning, even the smallest pivot will make an impact. Creating the smallest change in your life will affirm that you are heading in a better direction.

- Want to see how you would score? Go to PositioningTest.com

Chapter 10

Know Your Position: Self-Awareness

Find what gave you emotion; what the action was that gave you excitement. Then write it down making it clear so that the reader can see it too.
—Ernest Hemingway, American novelist and Pulitzer Prize Winner (1899 - 1961)

Know where you're going.
—Billy Wilder, American filmmaker (1906 - 2002)

Some of the world's greatest feats were accomplished by people not smart enough to know that they were impossible.
—Doug Larson, columnist and editor (1926 -)

Self-awareness is summarized by the fact that most of us do not see ourselves as other people see us. A movie clip from *Spaceballs* shows where Mel Brooks, who plays the role of the emperor, goes through the transporter which accidentally puts his head on backwards. He then looks down and says, "Why didn't somebody tell me my ass was so big?"

That is lack of self-awareness.

Most of us don't have a clue about ourselves.

Self-awareness is about becoming aware of who you are, what you do, and most importantly, where you fit.

When someone says they are going to take a certain course of action, and they know it is going to work for them because it worked for someone else—their rationale is erroneous. What might have worked for someone else doesn't necessarily mean it will work for you.

Whether it is getting an MBA or going out and joining a rock and roll band, all of us have to come to the point where we know ourselves well enough to realize that some goals may not happen. We all have constraints and different strengths and weaknesses.

In *The Art of War*, Sun Tzu summarizes self-awareness.

> **If you know your enemy and yourself you should not fear the outcome of one hundred battles. If you know yourself but not the enemy, for every victory gained you will also suffer a defeat. If you know neither the enemy nor yourself, you will succumb in every battle.**
>
> **—Sun Tzu, *The Art of War* Book III The Sheathed Sword**

Sun Tzu does not tell us that we will never lose, but that knowing yourself is as important as knowing your enemy, and that if we know *both* then we might lose a battle or two but we will win the war.

Most people are not self-aware because most prefer to know the external world instead of knowing themselves—the internal world. Knowing yourself, though, is incredibly important because all of positioning starts with whoever you are and wherever you are. Your position is later defined by what the other side perceives about who you are and what you are going to do, but *you* need to know that first.

The Power of Telling Your Story

I had a consulting client years ago, high tech guys, and they had built a great distribution business and were putting together a presentation for manufacturers so they could represent them and become their distributor. They knew all of the warts and errors of their own business. Their biggest pushback in putting this presentation together was how much they were going to disclose their limitations to the potential principals.

I advised them to focus on explaining who they were, and accent their strengths. It took several weeks to put this presentation together because of their decided lack of self-awareness, leading to self-consciousness and real fear that they were not able to master.

Once the presentation was finished, however, they delivered it and their success was measured in the fact that they went from thirty million to one hundred and twenty million dollars in three short years.

It wasn't that they were several times better than their competitors in many areas, but what they did have was a clear way to explain how they positioned themselves in a different and unique way.

If they had never solved that lack of self-awareness they would have never been selected to be the distributor. If you are wondering how you are going to be more successful, the first thing you have to understand is who you are. Let me give you a bonus right now:

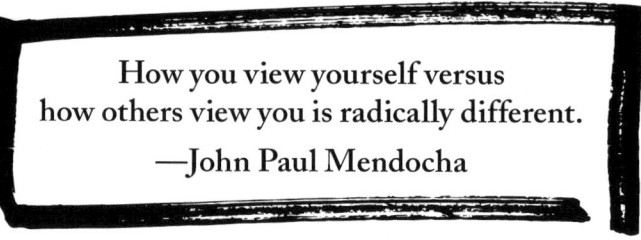

How you view yourself versus
how others view you is radically different.
—John Paul Mendocha

All too often people tell me that they think others are thinking about them one way or another. For the most part, unless you are positioned correctly or even positioned at all in their mind, chances are they are not thinking about you at all. Their focus is usually on themselves.

Self-awareness comes from critical thinking and Feedback Analysis, this is what we will concentrate on next.

A man's got to know his limitations.
—Clint Eastwood as Dirty Harry

Summary: Know Your Position: Self-Awareness

- Self-awareness is the first step. You must know what position you have before anything else.
- Lack of self-awareness leads to paralysis, lack of confidence and unclear messaging.
- Knowing yourself and knowing the enemy, according to Sun Tzu, are the two fundamentals of winning a war.

Chapter 11

Who Are You?

Who are you and how did you get in here?
I'm a locksmith. And, I'm a locksmith.
—Leslie Nielsen, as Lieutenant Frank Drebin,
Police Squad, (1982)

Raising the level of mediocrity is not a path to success.
—Peter F. Drucker, American management consultant,
founder of modern management (1909 - 2005)

The undertaking of a new action brings new strength.
—Evenius, ancient Greek legendary seer, circa 425 BC

Peter F. Drucker has been called the Father of Modern American Management, although he wasn't even born in the United States. He was born in Vienna, Austria in 1909, and moved to England before World War II. Eventually he moved to the U.S. and became a naturalized citizen.

127

He had an outstanding mind. He could look at a circumstance or situation, chronicle it, capture it, understand it and then very meticulously lay it out. I had the fortunate opportunity to see Peter F. Drucker live in the flesh seven times in my life. The first two times were billed as A Day With Peter Drucker in San Diego.

The first time I saw him in 1987, I was a lowly high-tech sales person for a fledgling company. The room was filled with over three hundred and fifty people from major companies; presidents, vice presidents, executives and high level staff who clearly understood the gravity of being in the same room as Peter Drucker.

I was already a fan of Drucker, having read all of his business books and studied his insights. However, I still felt like low man on the totem pole.

Drucker Insight for You

Drucker's incredible insight is the fact that most of us spend our lives, and harbor this belief, that when we look at ourselves, we find out what we are good at, we find what we are bad at and then all of our education, our energies, efforts and training are all driven to improve upon the *weaknesses* that we have. Thinking that we have bigger opportunities of growth where we are weak!

My burden lifted when Drucker explained that raising the level of mediocrity was not the path of success but only becoming a little less bad at whatever you are bad at. Instead, you have to build upon strengths. That was his insight, and Drucker provided that understanding to me.

I made significantly more progress, more success and more money because of that simple insight. Peter Drucker changed many people's lives, sadly very few people in the grand scheme of things got to see him live.

Others believe that he is old school and outdated. To my way of thinking, what makes Drucker different is that he understood the essentials. The Good, Bad and Ugly exercise which is inspired by Drucker will help you discover more about who you are and provides precious feedback.

Feedback Analysis

Whenever you hear people use the catch phrase, "I would just like some feedback," it is usually not completely sincere. Virtually no one just wants some feedback. What they want is a compliment, an "atta boy," or for someone to say you are validated and worthy.

All of those are important and may be even essential for your mental health. But for your success, what you really need is feedback that provides insight into what your strengths are. This opens the door to a higher level of self-awareness of your strengths and weaknesses. That will drive you to greater success.

If you can bare the realities of yourself, your competitors, your market and industry, then you are well poised to increase self-awareness and to grow. Most people do not want to do this. It was the German philosopher, Nietzsche, who said, "The measure of a man or woman is in the amount of truth he/she can tolerate."

We all fall victim to this, especially if you are thinking, "Oh yeah, that is true but only for *other* people, not for me." Then it is *definitely* true of you. And no wonder!

Who really wants the truth? Who really wants to find out how they are perceived by others? No one really. Yet, it is the *only* path that leads to success.

Only two things are infinite, the universe and human stupidity, and I'm not sure about the former.

—Albert Einstein (1879-1955)

Shortly before he died in 2005, Peter Drucker was celebrated by Business Week magazine as "the man who invented management." Naturally, when most people hear that description, they think of corporate management. And Drucker did, in fact, advise a host of giant companies (along with nonprofits and government agencies). But he came to his life's work not because he was interested in business per se. What drove him was trying to create what he termed "a functioning society." Drucker had, after all, seen firsthand what happens when society stops functioning.

In Cambridge, Drucker attended a lecture by leading economist John Maynard Keynes, and there had an epiphany: "I suddenly realized that Keynes and all the brilliant economics students in the room were interested in the behavior of commodities while I was interested in the behavior of people."

In 1946 Drucker met GM Chairman Alfred Sloan, who would in many ways become Drucker's model for the *Effective Executive*. "The chief executive must be... absolutely tolerant and pay no attention to how a man does his work, let alone whether he likes a man or not," Sloan told him. "The only criteria must be performance and character."

He also began his formal consulting practice and took on major assignments with Sears, Roebuck and IBM, among others. In 1954, he published *The Practice of Management*, widely considered the first book to organize the art and science of running an organization into an integrated body of knowledge. Before this, you could find books on individual aspects of managing a business—finance, for example, or human resources. But there was nothing that pieced it all

130

Peter Drucker

together. What was out there "reminded me of a book on human anatomy that would discuss one joint in the body—the elbow, for instance—without even mentioning the arm, let alone the skeleton and musculature," Drucker later recalled. By the time he began work on *The Practice of Management,* then, Drucker was, as he described it, "very conscious of the fact that I was laying the foundation of a discipline" In 1959 Drucker coined the term "knowledge work" foreshadowing a new economy where brains would trump brawn.

SOURCE: https://www.drucker.institute/perspective/
about-peter-drucker/

In 1999 Peter F. Drucker published *Managing Oneself,* a short article which appeared in the *Harvard Business Review* in 2008. In the article Peter Drucker explained that one of the hardest things to find out is one's strengths and yet as we already talked about, one can only build from strength.

He then goes on to say that one way to find out is to do an exercise that he calls Feedback Analysis.

We call this feedback analysis the Good, Bad and Ugly exercise.

Over the years I've looked at lots of different ways to log my time, discover more about myself and find out about the circumstances that surrounded me at that moment in my life. Unfortunately most of the exercises that I encountered turned out to be very complicated, almost impossible to do, and left me wondering what I just wasted my time on.

So I came upon this idea. Now I have to say that a client was already using an interesting variation of this, so I picked up the workable part. Remember always look for those things out there that work. And I developed what has become my Good, Bad, and Ugly exercise.

The exercise is designed to do a few things. It doesn't make you think about a dozen or a hundred things and it doesn't make you log every minute because, well let's face it, most of the population can't do that. I mean you can't get them to brush their teeth or floss or God knows what else, so how are they going to apply a very in-depth system?

Only Floss the Ones You Want to Keep

The purpose of doing a weekly Good, Bad and Ugly exercise is to provide feedback on your week. Our exercise uses a somewhat shorter way than what Peter Drucker talks about but it is the same idea.

We tend to forget many important life lessons. The tracking of these various events will make you more aware of what is going on in your life. By raising your level of awareness about your life you are taking positive steps to greater understanding.

Start to keep a weekly log of three good things, two bad things and one ugly thing that happens to you each week. That's it!

You *must* write it down. Our brain has the tendency to overlook, distract us or help us forget the bad, and particularly the ugly things that happen to us.

This exercise is not about dwelling on the negative, this is about getting feedback and learning even from the bad things that happen. You might even say, especially from the bad things.

Like pain, bad things that happen *are* feedback and feedback that should not be ignored. If something hurts and it won't go away, you might need to see the doctor. Pain is the feedback from your body to take action. Likewise, if there are things that you are doing that are painful and clearly not working, then you *must* take notice and do something different.

How Are You Going To Get Better When You're Stuck In A Maze?

So here's how the Good, Bad and Ugly sets up. First off you only really need six entries: three good, two bad, one ugly. In any given week you'll probably have more than that but you want to confine it. Prioritize it. When something good happens, write it down and say, "Hey this is something good that happened to me." Catch yourself having a success.

We wallow much too often in lamenting that things aren't going quite the right way. Or you hear people say, "I never get a break. Oh, when am I going to have my turn to win?"

But if I analyze their good, their bad, and uglies, I would find out every week they had some good along with the bad and ugly, because everyone has some of each. It's why there's a ratio. Now the bad needs to be included because when I originally started working with people about doing good, bad and ugly, I didn't have some rules and restrictions on it.

Now remember I'm not the boss of you. You have to

decide whether or not you're going to stick to my examples and my rules by acknowledging two things that were bad that happened this week along with the good things.

However, what I can tell you is that when people get crazy, they start exhibiting many different levels of bad. Everything that's bad that happens to them they wear on their sleeve and regurgitate it. Not a smart idea. There are good things that also happen every day.

Give an example of an ugly that happened and write it in the exercise in the book. Accept an ugly thing. Show exactly what this kind of thing looks like. Every week permit yourself to have one ugly. You should be able to figure it out. Put that in place and say, "All right there's my ugly."

Look at it. Don't do a lot of self-editing. Get it out of your head. You'll track a pattern. The filling out of the Good, Bad and Ugly exercise makes you aware of what's going on around you. It provides you feedback without tons of effort. What you'll find is that over time you'll get better at doing good, bad and uglies, and most importantly you'll understand that the feedback it brings you is going to pay back many times over the investment of time that you expended. You'll see a pattern emerge and an understanding of yourself, and even others. You'll be able to spot their own good, bad, and uglies.

The good, bad, and ugly concept really touched me because I am a big Clint Eastwood fan. *The Good, The Bad, and The Ugly* movie is quite an impressive feat. In my opinion, it's the best of the so-called spaghetti westerns that Clint starred in. That story is a metaphor for life. You have all three aspects. You don't just have the good. You don't just have the bad. You also have an ugly. All three are endemic. In life, well, you're always going to have a little bit of each, and the point of it is, what do you do with what you have?

So as you get the feedback from the exercise, it allows you to maintain an insightful perspective that generates growth. Growth happens by seeing and getting feedback.

Maybe you find that you have this recurring pattern of the same problem that comes up again and again and again. Now you have to say, "Can I fix this? Can I change this?" Maybe you can go in a different direction.

For me, the example is expense reports. I was so legendary at one company where I worked, they actually made a rule based upon me because of how late I was in getting them submitted. I really suck at getting expense reports finished. I had to develop a system.

Because I am still billing clients for expenses I incurred, the problem is the same. I *hate* doing expense reports. However, even if it costs me money, I pay somebody to get them done for me. Now I no longer have to deal with the tension and anxiety of expense reports. I bill clients promptly, and I stay more aware of what needs to be billed. Is it as good as it can be? No, but it's no longer an ugly. Most of the time, it's not a bad. In fact, it's good because we are billing more accurately and more rapidly.

The Good, Bad, and Ugly pointed out that I needed to have a strategy that would take care of that. I needed a coping mechanism by which I took this problem off my plate and removed it from my list forever. It hasn't shown up for many years because I have a system that takes care of it.

Anything that is that annoying, anything that is that problematic, anything that you cannot avoid, now it's time to figure out how to put it to bed once and for all. Learning to do that, getting that feedback from the Good, Bad, and Ugly means that you'll have more time for the best part of the life you want to live.

Sadly, most people never get to this point. One of my best friends is never going to get there no matter how many years he's going to live. Each day is a little bit like that movie, Groundhog Day; as they say, "Same old shit, different day." Frankly, I think that if he would use the Good, Bad, and Ugly and modify and change things a little bit here and there, what he would discover is one very important thing—his life can be better.

Your life can be better. All of us can learn from the feedback provided by the Good, Bad, and Ugly.

Feedback is what allows us to increase in self-awareness and what informs us of what works and what doesn't. What things do we need to do more and less of. What do we need to find solutions for, or try a different approach?

The question will always be:

How Much Truth Can You Tolerate?

To position to win in your life, it is essential to know and to see what is helping and what is not. As you collect this feedback using the exercises you will find things that need fixing, big and small.

Summary: Who Are You?

- Self-awareness is key because you need to know what your strengths are, because as Peter Drucker says, "You can only build on strengths."

- Feedback Analysis is one of the best ways in which you can objectively and methodically find what your strengths and weaknesses are.

- The Good, Bad and Ugly exercise is a simple and concise way in which you can keep track of the things that happen in your life and learn what things to do more or less of. The simple way to do this is using a 3-2-1 ratio—3 Good, 2 Bad, 1 Ugly.

- Download this form and other free materials at PositionToWinBook.com

Example of a Good, Bad and Ugly

Week Ending 06/09/19   On-site Client Work.

Good

1. Made it to client site without forgetting anything and had a great dinner meeting preparing for two days of strategy and analysis.

2. Discovered many levers that we are able to pull to bring the client out of bleeding out to a "Defensible Position" (Stage 1) where we can build a solid foundation for the Growth Stage (Stage 2)

3. Developed a 3 Month, a 6 Month and a 12 month plan of attack ranging from Sales process tightening to marketing campaigns (digital and physical) aiming at low hanging fruit.

Bad

1. Cash flow is a serious issue and we will have to renegotiate deals on behalf of the client fairly soon in the process to even have any resources towards a stabilization process.

2. There is major bleeding out and waste that is chronic and has weakened the business for a very long time. New hires will have to be hand picked and retrained according to new standards and held accountable.

Ugly

1. The client has unrealistic expectations of what his business is worth and this will be a considerable hindrance in the stabilization process because it will feel to him as "not good enough." Nothing dies harder than a dream that can never be.

POSITION TO WIN

Building a Better Position—Who Are You?

The Good, Bad & Ugly

Week of: _____

Week Starts: _____Sunday _____Monday _____Other

The Good:

_____

_____

_____

_____

The Bad

_____

_____

_____

The Ugly

_____

_____

_____

_____

Download this form and other free materials at
PositionToWinBook.com/FreeStuff

Notes

Chapter 12
Rock in the Shoe

Objects In Rear View Mirror
May Appear Larger Than They Are
—Side view mirror

We find no real satisfaction or happiness in life without
obstacles to conquer and goals to achieve.
—Maxwell Maltz, *Communication Bulletin for*
Managers & Supervisors, June 2004

It still holds true that man is most uniquely human when
he turns obstacles into opportunities.
—Eric Hoffer, American author, (1902 - 1983)

Growing up in Denver, Colorado meant that I was at the foothills of the Rocky Mountains. People would come from all over the country and stand in my backyard, look at those majestic mountains and say, "Wow, what a view." To me, it was just—well, it was my backyard.

Somewhere along the line, I became involved with the Boy Scouts, and our troop decided that we wanted to see how far we could push things to the ultimate award. We were not going to do just car camping and day hikes, but were going to achieve a level of expert—a level of attainment that very few people accomplished called the 50-Miler patch.

To receive the coveted 50-Miler patch, you carried everything on your back and walked for 50 miles, and camped along the way. This required certification of achievement.

The 50-Miler Boy Scout Award

The 50-Miler involved lots of arduous training to get into shape. When you're young, strong and energetic, you think that you're in pretty good shape, until you start to run for a mile. Then you find out that you become winded in just a little bit. But between bicycling like crazy and running every day, I eventually got into shape. The very first time our troop attempted the 50-Miler, in seven days we walked 79 miles in some of the roughest country that you would ever imagine—the Mount Zirkel wilderness area located in Routt National forest.

Mount Zirkel is the highest peak in the range at 12,182 feet named for Ferdinand Zirkel, a German geologist. All along the continental divide, we straddled this giant mountain range, walking our way from the south to the north, and achieved our end goal. We attained the 50 miles. Actually, the scout troop hiked 79 miles because we did get lost and go in the wrong direction here or there. Therefore, in all likelihood, we exceeded the 79 miles.

So here's what happens when you get up in the morning. You get your pack ready, put on your double pair of socks, your hiking boots, strap everything together, and then you put on a 55-pound pack. Then you are all ready to go.

Remember, we were carrying all the food that we were going to have for the entire week, and trust me, we were not going to end up leaving food in the pack. The first mile or so, you are feeling pretty good about the hike, but somewhere along the line, you'd end up kicking up a rock. Now, how a rock gets from underneath your feet up into the inside of your boot, I don't know. There must be some physicist or some geologist who can explain it to me, but it always ended up inside.

Stop the World! I've Got a Problem

Now, the first time it happens to you, you stop, you tell everybody else they have to stop, and you take off your pack, as painful as that is—because I'll tell you, once you get it off, you feel great, but all you know is, you've got to put the pack back on. You've got to keep walking, because you've got to make time. You take off your boot, balance yourself because there is nowhere to sit down, and you carefully take the offending rock out. The rock felt like this giant massive boulder, which weighed tons, but it wasn't that big. Over time, what you discover is that most shoe rocks were much smaller than you thought.

So often times, you'd find out that the smaller rocks, though annoying, would be just that, an annoyance that you would just have to learn how to live with. And you would walk with that rock in your shoe.

As I grew up, I understood that this rock-in-the-shoe is actually a metaphor for how most people go through life. They'll have an inconvenience, an annoyance, something that happens that aggravates them. They will stop on the side of the road, go through the arduous task of taking off the heavy load, finding a place to put it, taking off that boot, knocking the rock out and putting everything back together again and continue walking. But just a few hundred yards, sometimes a mile, sometimes all day, you'd have another rock in your shoe.

All of us have rocks in our shoes. All of us have inconveniences that hamper us. The question then becomes, how many rocks in the shoe do you have? Is it just an annoyance? Is it something that's slowing you down? Is it something that makes you stop? And, how big is it? You'd be surprised sometimes how small the rock is.

Some people stop every half an hour or even less and take rocks out of their shoes. Some scouts I'd look at and say, "That's just a tiny pebble, are you kidding me?" Now I'm not saying that you should walk around with a boulder in your shoe, but you have to have some level of understanding that everything in life has a certain kind of rock-in-the-shoe element to it.

How you deal with that will determine how far you go in life and how many times you stop. Every time you stop, it takes a lot of energy to get going again. When the scout

144

troop got to that 79th mile and walked to that base camp and took off our packs for the last time, now significantly lighter from food being eaten, every single one of us took off our boots and all of us had rocks in our shoes.

Duality of Success

We were relieved that we had completed the task. We were elated that we had achieved what most would see as unobtainable. I would go on to yet another 50-Miler, earn another patch and learned a lot about myself by going through that journey.

The process that we all go through is that journey. Stopping, though it may seem like the thing you need to do right now, is the very essence of destroying any chance that you will ever have of being very successful in your life. All of us have to overcome adversity, all of us have a rock-in-the-shoe. The question is, can you continue to move forward and understand that no matter what rocks in the shoes that you may have, that you'll never stop because there is no place at the top to actually sit down. It is always about moving on to that next step, and the next step, and the next. As you do that, you will see that accomplishments and, therefore, successes will become your life.

The Big Tuna

Romeo Crennel discovered one reason that Bill Parcells was ornery at practice. Before the coaches left their offices for one session, Crennel spotted the defensive coordinator placing a pebble inside his right sneaker, sliding his foot in, and tightly tying the laces. Parcells used the pebble as a "training mechanism" for staying alert. "Whenever I stepped the wrong way, it reminded me, 'Hey, be on top of this; pay attention," explains Parcells, who had started the peculiar habit at Florida State. "It was like having a little bell on your wrist: every fifteen seconds, it goes off." After practice Parcells placed the small stone on his desk with the rest of the collection from the practice field. His choice of stone size depended on his mood.

Parcells, Bill. Parcells (p. 57). Crown/Archetype. Kindle Edition.

Bill Parcells two-time winning Super Bowl coach

To Position To Win in your life, it is essential to know and to see what is helping and what is not. What is the constant rock in your shoe?

Not all problems, situations, or annoyances are created equal. Learn how to distinguish between what truly is vital, important, and what is only nice to have. Sometimes, one must live with what we have, to get to where we need to go. Do that and you'll understand the power of the story of the rock-in-the-shoe.

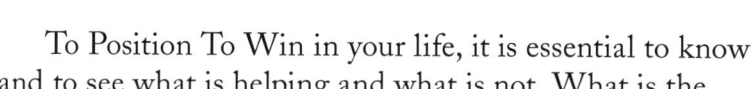

Learn how to distinguish between what truly is vital, important, and what is only nice to have.

—John Paul Mendocha

Summary

- Everyone experiences some level of rock-in-the-shoe in their life and business. It is always there—don't think that if you just did something different it would finally be gone.

- The key is always to be able to distinguish between what is:
  > Vital
  > Important
  > Nice to Have

- Develop the mental fortitude to endure the small and big problems as you work towards honing your current position or pivoting to a better one.

Notes

Chapter 13

Exploit Your Position: Self Acceptance

Acceptance is such an important commodity,
some have called it the first law of personal growth.
—Peter McWilliams, American self-help author from
Life 101 (1949 - 2000)

I define comfort as self-acceptance. When we finally learn that
self-care begins and ends with ourselves, we no longer demand
sustenance and happiness from others.
—Jennifer Louden, personal growth pioneer (1962 -)

Generally speaking, the way of the warrior
is resolute acceptance of death.
—Miyamoto Musashi, Japanese swordsman, philosopher,
strategist, writer and ronin (1584 - 1645)

Most of your life you fantasize about having that perfect
setup, where luck is in your favor, everything goes right, it

all just fits and you come out on top. You leave the arena with the crowd chanting your name and saying how well you've done and cheering you out the door. Few of us ever realize that kind of grandiose circumstance or situation.

My wife Rebecca and I had the wonderful opportunity to attend Super Bowl XXXII, the Green Bay Packers vs. the Denver Broncos. I had been a Denver Bronco fan since I was crawling, and Rebecca, who I met when she moved from Ohio to Denver to get her master's degree from the University of Colorado, became a dyed-in-the-wool, rabid fan, also.

The game was held at Qualcomm Stadium—previously Jack Murphy Stadium—in San Diego. Ironically, Phil Simms was in the booth with Dick Enberg and Paul Maguire. We had tickets in the southwest corner of the Broncos' end zone below the scoreboard.

The Packers were highly favored and were the defending champions. The Broncos had previously gone to the Super Bowl four times and lost four times; just like the Minnesota Vikings. In fact, the NFC had beaten the AFC in 13 consecutive Super Bowls.

The game was a nail-biter with the scoring going back and forth. Each team managed to score again and again.

Victory Delivered by Helicopter

In the second half, the Broncos were driving toward our end-zone and John Elway, the quarterback of the Broncos, was determined that they were going to score. The ball was snapped, he kept the ball, locked it against his side, began running, and jumped for the end zone. A Packer player hit him and he spun 360 degrees into our personal space. He made 8 yards, got a first down, and landed on the 5 yard line. First and goal. We screamed like banshees.

Chapter 13: Exploit Your Position: Self Acceptance

It was towards the end of the fourth quarter and the Broncos were ahead. We were on our feet and breathless with anticipation. I looked at Rebecca and she looked at me.

"We are going to win," I said.

She just grabbed my hand and squeezed. After so many years of suffering crushing losses and watching the Broncos lose Super Bowls, we were going to be vindicated.

In 1977 in Super Bowl XII, they lost to the Dallas Cowboys. The Broncos had Craig Morton, the quarterback with feet of clay, and a defensive team led by Tom Jackson and Lyle Alzado. The Dallas team had those incredible stars: Roger Staubach, Randy White, Too-Tall Jones, Tony Dorsett, and Thomas "Hollywood" Henderson. Coached by the ultimate coach, Tom Landry.

Then the Broncos achieved a return to The Big Game three more times in the seasons of 1986, 1987, and 1989. The defensive super stars were Karl Mecklenburg and Dennis Smith. The coach was Dan Reeves.

Rebecca and I were at the Rose Bowl in January of 1987 when they lost to the Giants with Phil Simms as quarterback, and didn't even have a chance in the second half of the game. And we were at Jack Murphy Stadium for Super bowl XXII when we watched Doug Williams of the Washington Redskins destroy us by throwing four touchdowns, become Super Bowl MVP, have the game of his life, and he was supposed to be a washed-up-has-been who beat us soundly after spraining his ankle in the first quarter.

Then Joe Montana and his 49ers literally annihilated us, chewed us up and spit us out, in January of 1990. Luckily we sat that one out.

But this time the Broncos didn't lose against Green Bay. Even though probably no one but Elway, coach Mike

Shanahan, and owner Pat Bowlen thought they were going to win. Elway finally had the monkey off his back, and the fans did too.

"Unfuckin' believable!" I yelled.

I called my father. I called my brother. And to think I almost took $3,400 bucks cash from a Green Bay Packer fan who lusted after the game.

Rebecca said, "No way! How would we feel if the Broncos win and we missed experiencing it live?"

We stayed at the stadium for 90 minutes after the game, just soaking up the ambiance, watching the presentation of the Lombardi Trophy, and singing *We are the Champions* by Queen.

An experience I will never, ever, forget. The indescribable joy of winning.

Super Bowl XXXII vs **January 25, 1998**
Denver Broncos   **Green Bay Packers**
       31   **24**

John Elway won on his fourth trip to the Super Bowl.
Attendance: 68,912

Terrell Davis: Most Valuable Player

"This one's for John." —Pat Bowlen, owner of the Denver Broncos

Being the Lead Dog Means Everyone Else Has One Single View

As the number one salesperson in several technology companies, I rarely had peers who were friends. I looked at them as peer competitors. We were all fighting for the same resources and for the same recognition and, frankly, I was fighting for commission dollars.

I wanted to be number one. I wanted to be that swing vote. One day after a sales meeting, we meandered into a bar and a mediocre sales guy named Rich could be heard very boisterously saying that if he had my territory and my great accounts, he could sell the crap out of them. Things would just fall into place. He would be number one. He would prove to everybody that he was that one individual who could take it to the top. He had all the pedigree that he needed.

A new manager came in and handed him a significantly better territory than mine, and now he had what he always said he wanted. Now he had his shot. Now he could prove everybody wrong about what a poor salesperson he really was. So for his sins, they gave him a shot.

He inherited this great territory, some established accounts, a wonderful forecast, and he salivated. He bragged. He talked about how much he was going to do and what vast sales were going to happen. He finally had the cards, and he was going to play the hand and prove to everyone what a giant among men he was. Sadly, this would not come to pass because Rich did not know himself. He did not know what he was capable of and what he wasn't. And frankly, he didn't know what his position was. He didn't even exploit his skills ansd talents. Sadly, he succumbed to the negative and mocked and derided the things that I was doing. The story ends with his dead body bouncing off of the pavement as yet another sales professional bites the dust.

153

Every Sharp Shooter Hits the Target in Their Mind Before They Pull the Trigger

Exploiting your position means knowing how to play to the best of your ability every single aspect of what you have in front of you. It does not mean that you will not have adversity, challenges and obstacles. It means that the better you become, the stronger you become. Also the more resilient you become, the better equipped you are. Then when you go out to exploit your position, you'll do the best that you possibly can, given the circumstances that you have. I've seen amazing results from those who understood that it's not necessarily the cards that you start with, it's the position and cards you end up with. Your ability to exploit that position is the best and fastest way to obtain success in this world.

Only a small fraction of us actually have that happen. Most likely, you encounter somebody and they say, "If only I had gotten this break, or if the cards had fallen my way." You are fortunate if luck, good fortune, or some fluke took place.

Whatever hand has been dealt to you, whatever your unique set of circumstances and capabilities and talents, that is what you have. It is your situation as of right now. It doesn't mean that it can't change. You are told hard work and effort will counter any deficiency that you may have; or finding the right partner and building the right team will take you into that new and better dimension. But that isn't what most of us do. What we do instead is squander our opportunities and wish that we had a better circumstance or situation.

Exploiting your position means that after you have spent the time to figure out who you are and have a better idea of what is going on in your life, you are then ready to step into action mode.

154

Overcoming Being-All-Dressed-Up With-No-Place-to-Go

What happens at this point, however, is that because of your increased self-awareness, the whole process can be daunting and even scary. This is exactly what our brains were shielding us from in the first place. Self-awareness comes with a price: fear and change. It is endemic.

Now you have to deal with the inevitability of who you are and where you fit in the universe and the reality and constraints that come with that awareness, to say nothing of all of the emotional weight that comes with that increased knowledge.

This is true of you whether you are looking at it from your personal side, your career, or your business. It extends to a product, a company, a market, an idea, a concept, an organization or an industry.

While these kinds of feelings and reactions are under-standable and normal, the place where you need to get to is the place where you can exploit your position, which is exactly what this is all about.

How do I take my position and use it to my advantage and put myself on the road to success? How do I make it work for me?

There is no better explanation of this process than the *Five Stages of Death and Dying* as described by Elisabeth Kübler-Ross.

We will call it the Five Stages of Self-Acceptance.

Denial

The first stage is, of course, Denial. You deny your position, which, by the way, we listed as one of the Barriers to Success.

You say things like:

"That isn't how I really am."

"That isn't who I really want to be."

This is the alcoholic who says, " I am going to quit tomorrow," or "I can quit anytime I want."

This is the abusive person who says, "I am sorry, it won't happen again."

Denial is a natural response but the risk is in remaining stuck in denial forever, which does happen, unfortunately.

Anger

After denial you get to the angry stage. You are angry about some revelation.

"I am not happy."

"I don't like the fact that my ass is so big."

"I don't understand this!"

So you go through a period of blame. Who can you throw this to? Is it my parents fault? My ethnicity? My bad luck?

The anger position—I'm right and the world is wrong. It's the difference between the two that makes you angry. Anger will be one of the biggest hurdles to getting to acceptance, but it is a process you must push through. But until you do, you will be stuck in anger where you will complain about things not being fair or say, "Why me?"

You don't take responsibility for your life and that makes you even angrier. It's like you're being a ball inside a pinball machine. You have no control.

156

Chapter 13: Exploit Your Position: Self Acceptance

How long will you stay in anger? For some people, it will be their whole life.

If You Think You've Got Something To Be Pissed About . . .

Woodstock
An Aquarian Exposition: 3 Days of Peace & Music
August 15-18, 1969

Look what happened to It's a Beautiful Day just before Woodstock. Their number one song was *White Bird*. But they didn't hear the word "Pull!" It got shot out of the sky in three seconds.

One white bird made it,
the other one didn't.

A Flip of the Coin, or,
How to Get Screwed in Less than 3 Seconds

A great example was the Woodstock Music Festival and promoter Bill Graham.

Michael Lang, an organizer of Woodstock, wanted the band, The Grateful Dead, to play, which at the time was represented by Bill Graham. Graham would let them play but he also wanted to take advantage of the moment and promote other artists he was associated with.

"Take The Grateful Dead, but I have two more bands that I want you to take."

The promoters said they were only going to take one more band. Michael Lang listened to both bands that Graham represented. He liked them both and couldn't decide so they flipped a coin. It's a Beautiful Day lost.

Santana won, and went on to become a star overnight.

Carlos Santana

It's a Beautiful Day was actually a pretty good group, but they are now a trivia question that would stump most. They had written a song called "White Bird". One is an icon of music history. The other an obscure reference.

Sometimes things aren't fair and anger is a natural response. We must realize that even if we don't get the lucky break we must push through the anger and get to action so we can keep moving forward to find that which will help our position.

Bargaining

Bargaining is a means to control and manipulate the situation to your best advantage. People try to negotiate with reality and come up with some kind of an exchange to deny reality.

This is seen in the disparity of results between different levels of negotiators. The best negotiators' results are not 3, 5 or 10% better, they are often measured in hundreds of percentages. This is true whether you are trying to get the best deal on a car, take over a business or exploit the human condition.

But no one can be in two places at the same time. You also cannot occupy more than one position at a time, unless you run a sub-atomic level business—and chances are, you don't.

All of the concepts in *Most Businesses Fail in the First 5 Minutes—It Just Takes Them 3 to 5 Years to Realize It* are useful and true because they line up with human nature and the constraints of physical reality. By trying to seek some compromise or some way to keep things the way they are, you are just delaying your progress. The longer you deny reality, the longer it will take for you to move forward.

The downside is that once you push through bargaining, you will grow sad and depressed. Take heart, as that is the last stage before true acceptance.

Depression

At this stage we don't want to accomplish anything. The lead singer of Warren, who wrote "Cherry Pie", grew sad and depressed to the very end of his life because he hated all that the song gave to him: the house in Malibu, the hot model, kudos for "Cherry Pie."

Depression is normal and part of the process. This is because you are realizing and fully embracing what and where you are, and you might not like it.

What you really have to do to exploit your position is to get past all the previous stages and get to Acceptance. Depression immobilizes you. You stop. Lack of formalized progress erects a roadblock. Many people can't get their head wrapped around moving forward. Concentrate on pivoting to your new position. Pivoting changes your trajectory.

Acceptance

Accept who you are and what you are. If you happen to be fifty-five years old and 100 lbs overweight in all likelihood you will not get a phone call that says, "Ted, we need you for the Olympic decathlon." That is simply not going to happen.

It doesn't mean that you can't improve your life. It doesn't mean that you can't knock off a few pounds, but first you must assess and accept where you are. Recognize who you are, what you can and cannot do, what position you have and take it from there.

Positioning is about improving your odds, changing your direction and altering the trajectory of where you are going but from concrete reality, not fantasy. Only then can you make positive, forward progress.

Self-acceptance is a very important part of exploiting a position. Often people will have success but they will have begrudging success. We see this in successful Internet companies. They are unhappy with the very product that makes them money, the very thing that is the source of their power and influence makes them upset.

Those Stinkin' Ads

Google

I met a man at a conference who worked for Google. How did I know he worked for Google? He was wearing a shirt that said Google on it.

I remarked, "Hey, that is a cool shirt! Where do they sell those?"

To which he promptly replied, "They don't, I work for Google."

By the way, I offered him forty dollars and he still wouldn't sell me the shirt. Which tells me he might not have been a capitalist, because that shirt was not worth forty bucks! However, I had enough self-awareness to know that I could talk him out of the shirt. He eventually gave me one for free.

When he asked me what I knew about Google besides what everyone else knew about Google, instead of the obligatory reply, I told him I had a client who helps people with Google Advertising.

He looked at me as if he had just bitten into a sour lemon and said, "Oh, those ads. I hate those ads!"

By the way, when he said it, ninety eight-percent or more of Google's revenue came from, "Oh, those ads. Those stinkin' ads."

If you can accept the position that you are in, you will win a significant battle. If you cannot accept the position you are in, you will always be dealing with internal conflict which will generate more heat than light, and diminish your capacity, energy and progress.

It All Starts With You

If you have self-awareness and a certain level of self-acceptance, you are now ready to take a further step in understanding that all positioning starts with Personal Positioning.

Think about people who stand out from the crowd, the billions of individuals who are out there: Steve Jobs, Mark Zuckerberg, Elon Musk, famous athletes like Michael Jordan, Lebron James, John Elway, actresses and performers, everyone who stands out from a point of personal positioning. Every business that is successful has some group of individuals who understand their own positioning, their own capabilities.

In the *Position to Win System* we have identified five categories which one can use to define personal positioning. Is this an exhaustive, all inclusive, 100% complete list? No, but it is the basis of success.

Most of you have not figured out how to go out and grow a bigger self.

A Bigger World for a Bigger You

An exercise from Ralph Waldo Emerson:

This is the way he liked to envision a bigger, larger world.

Stand up.

Close your eyes.

Hold your arms out from your sides a little bit.

Take a deep breath, and as you slowly release your breath, imagine a circle around you being the world that you are in.

Move your arms out a little more and visualize that whatever was beyond that circle was a bigger world and then mentally see the next ring out and the next ring out, imagining the ever greater expansion of the world around you.

What Emerson didn't talk about was the five dimensions that we believe are essential for anyone who is working to position themselves personally and even help anyone who you come in contact with. Remember the adage "Physician, heal thyself." Our version is, "Position Yourself." Know your starting place; know what and where that is so you can start from that position of strength.

No matter who you are and where you go, you are always defined by the position you have. Far too often people believe that position is something that occurs spontaneously when a ray of light comes down from above and taps your cranium and says, "You are this talented person," or "You are this driven individual."

History proves to us that having an edge or a deficiency in any one of these areas and having an understanding of the five dimensions will help you. But without judicious application in each and every area, you will always be hampered by the lack in any other area.

Miss one of the Five Dimensions and Lose Your Ear

Vincent van Gogh, the quintessential misunderstood genius, is a case in point. He had so much talent that it border-lined in madness. His genius was never truly rewarded in his lifetime; he committed suicide at the age of thirty-seven after decades of depression and failure.

Self Portrait with Straw Hat
Penniless in 1887; portrait worth
an estimated $80–150 million
at a 2013 auction

Raw talent is not enough. Even having the skills to translate his talents into works of art, and meeting and working with members of the French avant garde who helped him hone his style, was not enough to help Vincent van Gogh. It would seem that someone like that would *have* to be successful. Instead he is remembered as the incredibly talented genius who became an important influence with every painter who came after him, but who never got any recognition while still alive.

Don't be haphazard about working on all of the five dimensions of your personal position. Pay heed to the lesson of the blacksmith. He would start off banging the hot metal and he's got the big heavy hammer, forming the horseshoes and he keeps working on it. Every year his primary arm gets bigger and bigger because he's swinging a big heavy hammer. So he gets more and more out of balance as his other arm atrophies in comparison.

This points to what happens to when you only work on one of the five dimensions and you end up with this distortion that some may call grotesque. So avoid the Blacksmith Syndrome.

Can you visualize the next ring out from where you are? And the next? And the next? The Five Dimensions of Personal Positioning are how you can turn that mental exercise into a concrete reality.

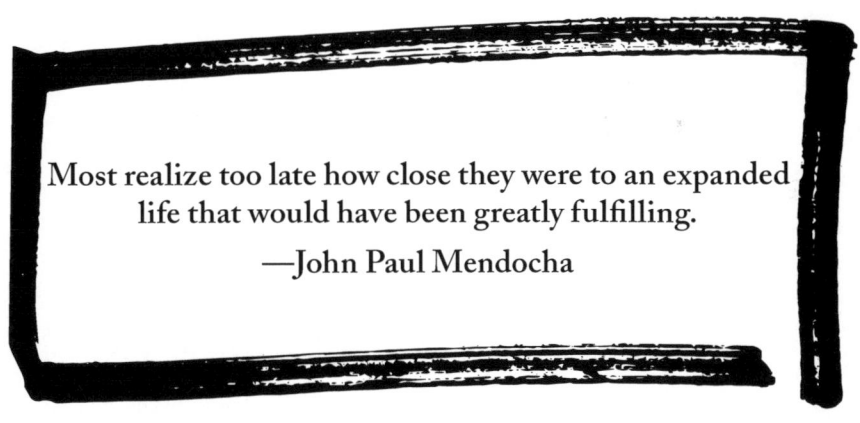

Most realize too late how close they were to an expanded life that would have been greatly fulfilling.

—John Paul Mendocha

Summary

- The first step to exploiting your position is Self-Acceptance. But even getting to self-acceptance is a process that requires you to go through The Five Stages of Self-Acceptance. It is the death of your beliefs about your shortcomings that moves you to a more powerful position.

- The five stages of accepting your position are adapted from Elisabeth Kübler-Ross, *On Death and Dying*.

- Denial

- Anger

- Bargaining

- Depression

- Acceptance

- The double-edged sword of talent is lack of awareness, underutilization of talent, and wasting your precious time not exploiting that talent. You would think that finding your talent would be easy—rarely is this the case. Most of us under-perform in the area in which we excel the most.

- Pay heed to The Blacksmith Syndrome.

Chapter 14

Five Dimensions of
Personal Positioning

Nothing endures but personal qualities.
—Walt Whitman, US poet (1819 - 1892)

Personally, I'm always ready to learn,
although I do not always like being taught.
—Sir Winston Churchill, British politician (1874 - 1965)

The secret of concentration is the secret of self-discovery. You
reach inside yourself to discover your personal resources, and
what it takes to match them to the challenge.
—Arnold Palmer, US golfer (1929 -)

Positioning starts with you, and we mean this literally, with you as an individual. Although you can, and should, apply these concepts at all levels of analysis, this chapter is about the Five Dimensions of Personal Positioning.

Don't be haphazard about working on all of the five dimensions. Do that and what you will be is a person who never lived up to their potential. Personal positioning is about finding out what your potential is with your eyes open. Seeing that the world is not a place that is continuously closing in on you, but instead a world that expands to match the ambition that your position allows. Success is obtaining that position.

The idea is to start gathering data and feedback along these five dimensions to discover who and where you are.

The five dimensions are:

Talents

Education

Skills

Experience

Resources

We all have a certain set of Talents, Education, Skills, Experience, and Resources at our disposal. The problem many times is that we believe that a different set of talents or education or skills are what we need to get us to where we want to go.

Here is the Bad News

Acquiring talents is next to impossible. Developing skills, experience and education is time consuming and expensive. On top of that, if you build from weakness the best case scenario would be to go from bad to mediocre. The worst case scenario would be an abject failure.

Here is the Good News

What you have *now* is enough to get you started!

As Peter Drucker said, "One can only build from strength." And chances are you have strengths and capabilities that are dormant or underutilized right now.

> We all have a vast number of areas in which we have no talent or skill and little chance of becoming even mediocre. In those areas a knowledge worker should not take on work, jobs and assignments. It takes far more energy to improve from incompetence to mediocrity than it takes to improve from first-rate performance to excellence.
>
> —Peter Drucker

Take off your rose colored glasses

Do you have the courage to acknowledge your latent set of Talents, Education, Skills, Experience, and Resources? Most people are wrong about what these are and even those who know, undervalue their own set of characteristics and believe they need to become a different person to be successful. Again, this is very difficult if not impossible to do. Many people never accept their capabilities and live a diminished life.

So how do you find out what you don't know that you don't know?

> "I never know what I think about something until I read what I have written on it."
>
> —William Faulkner

Feedback Analysis

> **Feedback drives all human behaviors.**
>
> —Tom Meloche

Use the following descriptions and questions to start to map out what your Five Dimensions of Personal Positioning are. Start to double down on the things you do well and find solutions for the things that you are not great at.

We have included descriptions that will help clarify individual aspects of your life and how you can start to analyze what is already giving you results and what is standing in the way.

Too many people believe that the way to improve is to get better at what they are bad at. They believe their opportunity lies in what they have a hard time doing, or what they can't do at all. People believe that with more education, more experience, more of this, more of that, *then* the world will beat a path to their doorstep.

If you are one of those individuals and are always looking for that next thing, read on.

For those who have worked towards acquiring a new set of knowledge check marks or experiences and are wondering, "Now what?" Read on.

For those who have acquired what you were told was necessary, but have found first hand that even though you fit the bill, you still don't have those opportunities that you desire, read on.

The first step is to go through the five dimensions and start to make a list of each. Once you have your lists, then you can start working on how to use your strengths *for* you and find solutions to your weaknesses. Like getting someone else to do what you are weak at, for example. Then you can begin to move forward with purpose, focusing on the things that you know will give you the greatest return.

> Man is very well defended against himself . . . The
> actual fortress is inaccessible, even invisible to him, unless
> his friends and enemies play the traitor
> and conduct him in by a secret path.
> —Friedrich Nietzsche

Focusing on what you naturally do well and what you already have, or even what will take a relatively short time to acquire, will be the most time effective and powerful lever that you can use in your personal positioning. Then you can position yourself to win.

Every person has at least some level of all these five dimensions. We are going to map them one by one, first by getting to know what these are and how they differ. Then later by noticing them and writing them down in our daily lives.

Personal Positioning Map

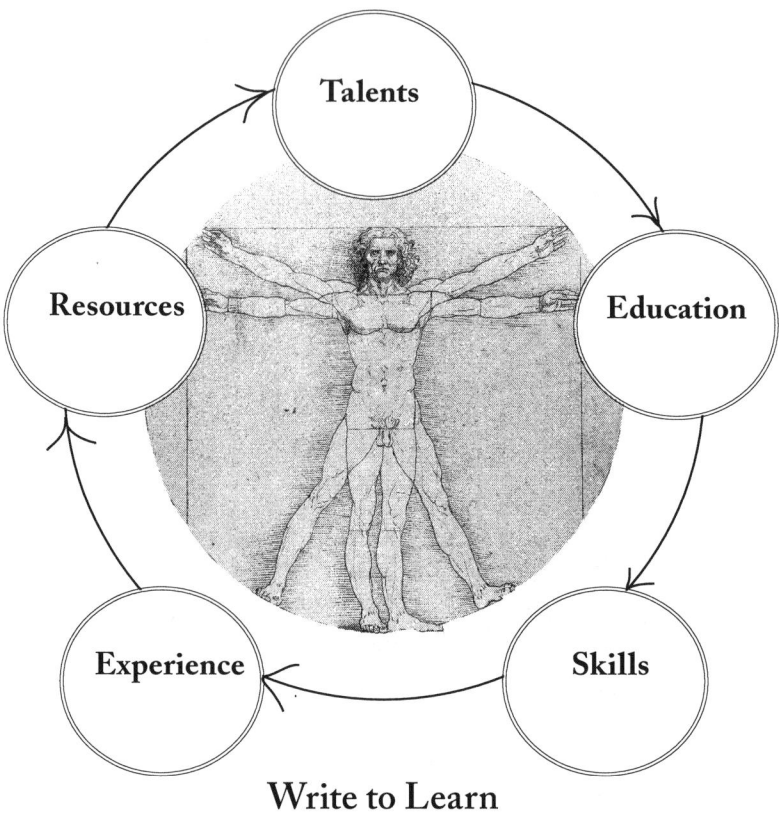

Write to Learn

The challenge here is that any step towards self-awareness can be uncomfortable and even painful. Our brain is constantly guarding us against knowing too much about ourselves.

> To defeat the enemy within, we will use the
> ancient art of writing things down!
> —John Paul Mendocha

You will be amazed at how much things change when you write them down and reflect on them later, when you are in a different state of mind. Because your brain has distracted you and hidden the details from you, reading what you wrote will reveal undiscovered aspects of yourself.

> **Writing is easy. You just open a vein and bleed.**
> —Ernest Hemingway

Summary

- The first step towards personal positioning is to recognize and gain awareness over the Five Dimensions of Personal Positioning:

    Talents

    Education

    Skills

    Experience

    Resources

- Your mind is an "inaccessible fortress", as Nietzsche says. To that end, we must use the analytical approach to find our way in.

- Our primary aid in self-analysis will be to write things down. Writing things down makes Feedback Analysis objective and useful.

Notes

Chapter 15
Talents

Having talent is like having blue eyes.
You don't admire a man for the color of his eyes.
I admire a man for what he does with his talent.
—Anthony Quinn, American actor, painter, writer and
film director (1915 - 2001)

If you hear a voice within you saying "You are not a painter,"
then by all means, paint ... and that voice will be silenced.
—Vincent van Gogh, Dutch post-impressionist painter
(1853 - 1890)

Do not go where the path may lead.
Go where there is no path, and leave a trail.
—Anonymous

Talents are really sneaky. They hide in plain sight. We take them for granted and deny their existence. We ignore their power and often work at cross purposes to our best interests. Because certain things come easy to us, we project that everyone must have the same level of talent. We dream that if only we could possess some magic to conjure up those childhood fantasies of being omnipotent. However we should realize that the face staring back at us in the mirror every day, has all the talent that we could ever need.

Talents are gifts. Things that you naturally and consistently do well with little to no effort. These are the most invisible of all and more than likely undervalued by you. They are by definition ordinary to you, because they are you. Your talents are done easily, frictionlessly and elegantly: Ted Williams hitting a baseball. Michael Jordan tossing up a basketball. John Elway executing the Drive in hostile Cleveland Browns' territory. Tiger Woods hitting a hole-in-one. Lewis Hamilton driving a Formula One car.

What is important to remember is that your talents are not ordinary to other people. Pay attention to what people say about you, the little comments and compliments. Even the negative things. In there you will find clues as to what your talents are. Here are some other things to help you find out what your talents are. Don't forget that you will be writing these down.

Things You Can Do to Find Out What Your Talents Are

Pay attention to what annoys you about other people. That can be a clue of something that you are extremely good at and, therefore, annoying that you can do it so much faster, better or more efficiently.

It could also be a clue of something that you, yourself

do, and therefore annoying. You see yourself reflected in others and who likes that? Except we are looking for things about us, so always write those down.

Pay attention to things you get in trouble for. Why did you get in trouble as a kid growing up? Comedians who are naturally funny would show off in the classroom to the exasperation of their teachers but to the delight of the other students.

Growing Up in Comedy with Dan Levy

by Isaac Kozell vulture.com/Isaac Kozell
November 17, 2016

Kozell:
I think anybody that's followed your comedy career probably has a sense that they've grown up with you in terms of the evolution of your material.

Levy:
That is totally true. That's funny, especially look-ing at my hour special because the first real jokes I ever did were about how I love buying condoms. I wrote that joke when I was 19. The whole joke was that if you're buying condoms you're having sex and if you're having sex you're awesome. It wasn't a great joke. Now my special is like, "I have two kids. I guess I never really used those condoms that I bought at CVS in 2001."

Kozell:
Can you return them?
Levy:
Yeah, they're still in the box.

———————— ◆ ————————

When you got in trouble for doing these things, they were natural activities and, although they might have been expressed in the wrong context, the wrong time or the wrong way, they hide a natural ability. Can you generalize the specific instance on what things you got, or even still get in trouble for, to come up with something that you are naturally good at?

What do you get in trouble for at work?

What gets you in trouble with your significant other or with friends?

Again, these are not necessarily good things but they can hide strengths. They simply need to be brought to the right context. Like being stubborn might be a bad thing in some contexts, like in a relationship, for example. But that can be a sign that you are a person who doesn't give up, who is tenacious.

Pay attention to when people tell you the following things:

"I think you missed your calling."

"You are in the wrong job."

Most of the time people say these kinds of things half joking and half serious. But what is really happening is they are seeing in you something that you are doing that doesn't quite fit, and they are letting you know that it is good. Make a note of it.

Right Person, Wrong Occupation

Bob Newhart worked as an accountant for United States Gypsum before he became a comedian.

He later said that his motto, "That's close enough," and his habit of adjusting petty cash imbalances with his own money, shows he did not have the temperament to be an accountant. He also said he was a clerk in the unemployment office who made $55 per week, but who quit upon learning unemployment benefits were $45 a week and he only had to come into the office one day a week to collect it.

Pay attention to what subjects you are naturally interested in.

- What topics do you own more than a few books about that are outside of the field where you actually work or have experience in?

- What are the subjects that capture your imagination? Note the ones you end up watching long hours of YouTube videos and Netflix documentaries, or topics you research on the Internet for the fun of it.

Pay attention to what you repeatedly fail at or what you have to force yourself to do every time.

- Is it starting things?

- Is it finishing things?

- Do you like working with your hands? Or do you hate it?

Realize There are Guys Who Make a Living Juggling Chainsaws

Do you like thinking conceptually? Or do you prefer working off a checklist? Things that are expected of you in your job or profession provide insight into who you are. This is not a fool-proof method, but sometimes something that we have to force ourselves to do is actually a strength on the opposite side of that same spectrum.

Job descriptions and profession specifications are not written with individuals in mind. There might even be a need in your particular situation to move responsibilities from you to other people while you take on other work that you are better suited to. Most companies are making a mess of their own human resources by not understanding this, but that is a whole other book.

Observe the deadlines you always miss, the things your wife or husband or other family members are always complaining to you about. Again these can be strengths on the other side of the continuum.

For example, if you always forget to work on that home improvement project that your wife has been asking you to do; you might realize that you don't enjoy working with your hands. Which probably means that you are more of a thinker, even an abstract thinker who thrives in strategizing. Now you can strategize about how to get someone else to fix that leaking faucet because you sure as hell are not going to do that!

Ask people close to you in the different circles that you live in—family, work, hobbies, friends—to tell you what they think you are naturally better at doing than most people.

Those are just some ideas of what to pay attention to and what to start to write down. As you make a note of these, you will start to see patterns that you can test. You do this by doing more of the things you are good at. Also by doing less, or nothing at all, of the things that you are not good at. Then see if this gives you even better results.

Finding your talent is all about catching yourself doing things that were almost effortless, seamless and far too easy. Talents often hide in plain sight and we take them for granted, unaware that what we're doing is nearly impossible for others. Watch yourself from the corner of your eye and see the talent that is in you.

First, there must be talent, much talent. Talent such as Kipling had. Then there must be discipline. The discipline of Flaubert. Then there must be the conception of what it can be and an absolute conscience as unchanging as the standard meter in Paris, to prevent faking. Then the writer must be intelligent and disinterested and above all he must survive. Try to get all these in one person and have him come through all the influences that press on a writer.

The hardest thing, because time is so short, is for him to survive and get his work done.

—Ernest Hemingway,
Green Hills of Africa

Summary

- Talents are innate—you can't change talents any more than you can change your eye color.

- Your talents are invisible to you—they seem ordinary and of little value.

- Use the questions in the Position to Win, Building a Better Position—Talents questionnaire as a start to find out what your talents are.

- Go to PositionToWinBook.com/freestuff to download a printable version of the questionnaire.

POSITION TO WIN

Building a Better Position—Who Are You?

TALENTS

1. What things annoyed you about people this week?

_____

2. What subjects interested you this week? Things you read about or came across that you thought were interesting?

_____

3. What did you get in trouble for this week?

_____

4. What compliments did you receive this week? What were they about?

_____

5. What did you fail at this week? What things could you not get done or even started?

_____

6. What deadlines did you miss? Can you remember if you have missed deadlines like this before?

_____

7. Ask a family member or close friend or colleague to tell you something they think you naturally do better than most people.`

_____

8. What did you procrastinate about this week? What did you pawn off on somebody else?

_____

Download this form at https://PositionToWinBook.com

Chapter 16
Education

I think of all the education that I missed.
—Van Halen, musician (1955 -)

*Education's purpose is to replace an empty mind
with an open one.*
—Malcolm Forbes, in *Forbes* magazine
US art collector, author, & publisher (1919 - 1990)

Education is a progressive discovery of our own ignorance.
—Will Durant, US historian (1885 - 1981)

When you hear the word education, the spring-loaded traditional thought is a formal one loaded with diplomas, certificates, Ivy League schools, and lots of brickwork. But education is not limited to the strict enclave of formal education. It includes informal education, online education and even the School of Hard Knocks.

In reality, you are educated by your experiences and from life itself, if you manage to stick with it and learn the lessons that this school can teach.

When Peter Drucker was asked what he thought about the school of hard knocks, he promptly responded:

"The problem with the school of hard knocks is the dropout rate. Too many people enroll in it but they either drop out and stop learning or never learn the lessons in the first place."

How true!

Failure *can* be a good teacher but it is far from ideal. No one has the time to make all the mistakes they need to make in order to learn. So to avoid that, we should learn vicariously from other people's mistakes. Education is about finding the target that you can actually hit without too much trial and error.

> **The faintest ink is more powerful than the strongest memory.**
> **—Chinese proverb**

In this section, use the form to write down schools you have attended and also programs that you have enrolled in and certificates acquired. It should be pretty straightforward and easier than the previous exercises. Write down what diplomas you have and if you have a certain set of letters after your name. This is most traditionally what people associate with who you are.

Chapter 16: Education

Write down training or certifications acquired, even if it is not in the field you work in or is in a field you desire to work in.

A word here is in order. If you have read this far and have connected some dots, you will start to see why an education from the right school or having a PhD is important, because it obeys the Rules of Positioning. We do not mean to be cynics here. Surely there are many sincere, dedicated and talented people who have graduated from all kinds of schools.

But someone from Harvard or Yale will always get extra points, at the very least, in the mind of the person they are trying to persuade, compared to someone who graduates from an unknown school. The person with the Ivy League degree might get the job or opportunity just based *soley* on the fact that they have the right school on their resume. This too obeys the Rules of Positioning.

Remember this is just a piece of a much bigger puzzle that is positioning. Especially because education, by definition, is still only a means to an end.

Education is an asset, so if you happen to have a law or business degree from a top university you might want to use those in your favor. But if you don't, then you should work around that, unless you are prepared to spend the money and the time to get a degree. Even then, if you decide to get a degree, it doesn't guarantee you anything. You would still have to go back and work on your positioning which would bring you right back here.

Two travelers are sitting in an airport lounge.

Bob: Do you know how you can tell that an MBA is losing an argument?

Sally: No, I don't.

Bob: They tell you where they went to school.

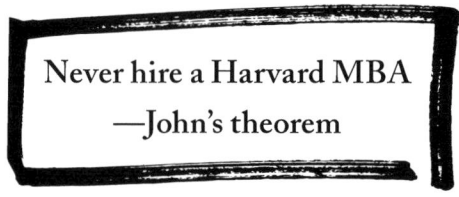

Never hire a Harvard MBA
—John's theorem

As prestigious as a Harvard MBA degree is, I find that the people who have one, have a hard time dealing with the realities of the marketplace, and are less effective than salespeople who don't have a degree. I've encountered not one, not three, but five Harvard MBAs in the course of my career. Two of them were clients, three of them I either worked with or worked for. Unfortunately, all of that training at Harvard created a mental state which made them less effective than they potentially could have been.

Implementing The Sharp Edge of Marketing

So when I became a consultant and speaker, I came up with a speech where I stated, "Never hire a Harvard MBA." When I delivered it to an audience of about 300 people, it was interesting to see the reaction in the room. It was applying the principle which is called using The Sharp Edge of Marketing. With this technique you eliminate as many maybes as possible, and either have solid no's, or absolute yes's.

The Sharp Edge of Marketing means you make a startling statement that has a sharp edge and that will tell you who will agree with what you say, and those who won't—attraction and repulsion. Both are important.

When I say, "Never hire a Harvard MBA," I mean it, because when I had worked with or worked for Harvard MBAs, they had a certain mindset that assumed a pie-in-the-sky plan that would magically make sales happen. They never seemed to have their feet on the ground. Most of these Harvard MBA guys are talking in platitudes and utopian outcomes and are very seldom successful salespeople.

I quickly flash backed to my firemanship merit badge—when you make a fire you need oxygen, fuel, and heat in the correct ratio and proportion, and you'll end up with fire. The Harvard MBAs appeared to want to put those elements close to each other, stand back, fold their arms, and watch.

Contrarily, I knew that one had to dive right in. To make a fire one has to work as vigorously and as hard as possible to get a fire started, even though you have all the conditions that are right to provide that spark.

Harvard MBAs believe in spontaneous combustion, which is very rare in nature, and even rarer in business. Waiting for something to happen versus absolutely busting your ass to make it happen, well, you have to bust your ass, that's just the way it goes.

Rarely Does an MBA Have a 9 Mil

By using that highly controversial "never hire" remark, I would be able to divide the room into those who found that abhorrent and those who agreed with me, and found it a wise thing to say.

Essentially I could eliminate the never-buyers and most importantly, be able to talk to only those who would be my best prospects—those who would understand the bottom-line thinking that I had. They would know the mind set that I have, that for any business to be successful, one has to do everything feasible with those three elements of fire— fuel, heat and oxygen—and work as hard as you possibly can to make that combustion.

And sure enough, as I finished my presentation and as I was walking off stage, I saw three people approach me rather rapidly. One of them I could almost pick was going to be the Harvard MBA. Two of the others said, "Thank God. You finally told the truth."

The Harvard MBA thanked me for pointing out to him that he had to work smarter to be successful.

Now, don't get me wrong. You can learn a lot from the courses from Harvard, and from all of the business schools: Wharton, Stanford, and many others. But what you have to understand is never hire a Harvard MBA, unless you know that that person is action-oriented.

When you're out positioning yourself to win and you say you're going to get an MBA, understand what you're going to do with that MBA. That MBA is not an end in itself. In some ways, it's barely a means to an end. What it is, is a start. It's a door opener. It's a positioning statement. It plugs you inside of somebody's head. If they believe that you having an MBA is the most important thing, life is good. If they don't, life isn't as good as it could be.

A Round Peg in a Square Hole

All of positioning has to do with finding how you fit in the prospect or in the other person's mind. Now, don't get me wrong. An MBA has value. Many people will pay you more if you have an MBA. But never believe that just because you have one, that you can just coast and sit on your ass and success is going to spontaneously happen. Never hire a Harvard MBA, because they are very expensive and they may not produce the results you want; therefore, my mindset is why risk it?

Jeff Bezos had a degree from Princeton University and eventually got a lucrative job at a hedge fund company before starting Amazon.

The question is, how much do you think his Ivy League education helped him start Amazon? Maybe the right thing to do is to do exactly what Jeff did. Go out and get an Ivy League degree and then start an online retail store. Except there already is a Jeff Bezos, and an Amazon. If you were to start your own version of Amazon from scratch, how far would you go?

Unless you are completely delusional, you probably realize that is a moon shot compared to using what you already have. Don't assume that what worked for someone else will work for you. That's one of the biggest mistakes in positioning.

No matter what level of formal education you have, you will benefit from doing all of the exercises in this book, since they will refine the way you think about education and your other assets. This will point you towards the shortest path to a better position.

Better School, Better Person?

Education is not only about capability. If it was, then an MBA from Harvard or Wharton would be worth the same as an MBA from the University of [Name your State], or from an online university. Suppose that they both would have the same curriculum, teach the same courses and both degrees are in Business Administration. Still the MBA from the University of Phoenix is just not as plum as an MBA from Harvard.

It is more important if you can match your education to your personality and other resources that you already possess. But what you have is enough to get you started because education is not the only thing important as you position yourself to win. Work towards converting education into knowledge and use that knowledge to leverage yourself into the best position.

Work is a Four Letter Word

To get to the top 20% in any field, read, read, read!

Do you want to become an expert in almost any field in a short period of time? It's not easy and will require that four letter word—work. Pick the field that you want to be an expert in. Use Google and Amazon to map out five to twenty books that are on that specific topic. At your own risk, read the top level article that shows up on Google search, knowing that it may be misleading. That is your starting point. With each additional book that you read be careful that you don't fall into the trap of confirmation bias. That is, with each new book you look for only that which matches what you have already read. Your task is to expand your knowledge in this field.

Don't expect that you will be a bona fide expert, but you are well on your way to reaching the 60-80 percentile level about that subject.

My own example when I started my first business at fifteen was to read a book about the mail order business. By the time I read a half dozen of them and I started to apply this information, my knowledge expanded and the concepts fell into place.

Today all these years later when a new and exciting field breaks out, I use a modified version of this strategy.

Take heart. In many years, up to twenty-five percent on the Forbes 400 list have a high school diploma or less.

It's important that you include all the education that you have received from any source. The real power will be in laying out all your assets and deficiencies and seeing the patterns in the fabric of your life.

Summary

- Education is most traditionally what people think about when they get asked the question, "Who are you?"

- Remember education is only a piece of the bigger puzzle that is your personal positioning.

- Although, if you do happen to have a good degree from a top university, your task is to line it up with the other four dimensions.

- Write down all the certificates and training that you have had and organize a time-line. This process might also be helpful in filling out the other four lists.

- Use the questions in the Position to Win, Building a Better Position—Education questionnaire to help you fill our your education.

- Go to PositionToWinBook.com to download a printable version of this questionnaire.

POSITION TO WIN

Building a Better Position—Who Are You?

EDUCATION

1. List schools you have attended.

_____

_____

2. List degrees that you have

_____

_____

3. List certificates that you have

_____

_____

_____

_____

4. List courses or classes you have taken to learn things. List the ones you remember even if they seem like they wouldn't fit with anything you are doing now. Make a complete picture of yourself.

_____

_____

_____

_____

_____

5. List any other training or licenses you might have; perhaps you have a real estate or insurance license or you studied to take a test of similar sort.

_____

_____

POSITION TO WIN

Building a Better Position—Who Are You?

EDUCATION

6. Informal education like seminars and workshops.

_____
_____
_____
_____
_____
_____

7. Books you have read, audio you have listened to, videos you have watched, and games you have played.

_____
_____
_____
_____
_____
_____
_____

8. School of hard knocks: anything you have had to learn through experience, under live fire with bullets coming in.

_____
_____
_____

Notes

Chapter 17

Skills

Nothing is more sacred to a craftsman than his equipment,
and no one can tell you which are the best for you.
—Kenneth Atchity, American producer, author
and columnist (1944 -)

When love and skill work together, expect a masterpiece.
—John Ruskin, English critic, essayist, & reformer
(1819 - 1900)

Let each man pass his days in that wherein his skill is greatest.
—Sextus Propertius, Elegies, Roman poet (55 - 16 BC)

Skills represent an area that you can consciously effect in the shortest period of time. They are acquired and cumulative, and can somewhat overlap talents but don't necessarily have to.

Think of a child who learns how to read in the first grade. When they are encouraged and develop the skills necessary to read at a higher level, they will rapidly advance in school. Conversely, those who just get by, rarely receive the highest rewards. Applying this to any area of specialized knowledge, means that in less than 18 months, you can become an expert in a particular field of study. Develop baseline skills and you will be able to leverage your talents to the maximum.

Given the enormous reach and power of the Internet, mark out a course of action, define what skills you will need, how your position will be affected and how you will pivot to an even better position in the near future.

It always starts with selection. Make sure you pick those skills that support, build and bolster your position. If you have no aptitude in a particular area, it is better to consciously abandon it, develop a coping strategy to take care of it, and focus your energy on those areas that will provide you with the positive feedback of success that will serve as a motivator for you to sustain your efforts.

For example, you can have skills in areas you have little talent, which makes them not very useful. Also, you may not have skills in things where you actually have a high degree of talent. This can happen often because you have never had to develop special techniques to be able to take advantage of that talent, since you have a natural aptitude.

Imagine if you could match both skills and talent. That is a prescription for success.

How You Can Learn a lot from Flickering Images

When I attended the Montessori school on crack, we were given the opportunity to develop some of our own courses. I picked the film industry because I already enjoyed

196

watching movies and thought what could be easier? You go to a theater, you get some snacks, you sit your ass down, you watch a movie. It turns out it's a little more complicated than that.

And then, I became intensely interested in how this incredible communications method had evolved—some years seeing upwards of 150 films. When someone today asks me how did you become an excellent storyteller, I tell them to watch these master storytellers, and absorb their methods. Though I've never written a screenplay (virtually everyone in southern California has one in the back of their mind or car), I have learned a lot about how motion pictures are made, which has significantly enhanced my marketing skills. The power of developing these skills, is that skills are not linear, you may take a circuitous route. In all likelihood, my skills were a hidden, unfair advantage to my competition throughout my career.

Things You Can Do to Find Out What Your Skills Are

Think about the training you have had in the past, even if it seems unrelated to what you are doing, or what you want to do. Many times we learn things in other areas of our life that seem like they don't apply but, they can be combined or included in what we are doing or want to do. So write them down.

Did you learn a new language because you moved to a different country or get training on software because you were filling in at work? Or maybe while involved with hobbies or travels you learned something most people are not privy to. Make note of that.

Possibly because of your family background you had experience in a particular industry or learned specific skills on a type of machine, or software, or managing people, or putting reports together. Skills can be hiding in a myriad of places. Just because you have the talent doesn't mean you have the skills necessary to accomplish and achieve your potential. Paradoxically, those who have few talents can still develop and obtain skills and often out-perform someone with superior talent. Sadly many people with a whole lot of talent never achieve success and squander their innate ability.

The idea here is to start to collect these skills and layer them over your talents. Do they overlap, or are they in conflict?

The more we line up all the aspects of our five dimensions and keep honing them, the better tools and techniques we will have to pivot to a better position.

Summary

- Skills are developed over time, and they accumulate. They can be the diligent application of talents or the haphazard process of learning to do things.

- Skills are any training or things you know how to do. You might know how to do it really well, or barely at all. Still take the time to write them all down.

- Use the questions in the Position to Win, Building a Better Position—Skills questionnaire to help you fill out what your skills are.

- Go to PositionToWinBook.com to download a printable version of the questionnaire.

POSITION TO WIN

Building a Better Position—Who Are You?

SKILLS

1. What are the languages that you speak ?

_____

2. List software programs that you know how to use.

_____

_____

3. List machines that you know how to use.

_____

_____

4. Think about industries that you have worked in or that you have background in (through family, school, or prior work, for example). Have you learned any skills relevant to that?

_____

_____

_____

5. What other skills do you have?

_____

_____

Download this form at https://PositionToWinBook.com

Notes

Chapter 18

Experience

Never regret. If it's good, it's wonderful.
If it's bad, it's experience.
—Victoria Holt, English author (1906 - 1993)

If you have made mistakes, even serious ones, there is always
another chance for you. What we call failure is not the falling
down, but the staying down.
—Mary Pickford, Canadian-born American film actress
and producer (1892 - 1979)

Good judgment comes from experience.
Experience comes from bad judgment.
—Anonymous

It has been said that experience is the best teacher.
However, few capture the lessons and build off the insights
that are provided.

Experience can be elusive and invisible to you as it blends your memory and mind with your own identity. Also, bad experiences and mistakes that you have made can quickly fade away in your memory as your mind tries to help you forget the pain associated with it.

However, if you were to ignore the bad experiences and the mistakes you make, then that time would *really* be wasted. If you don't learn why you made the mistakes that you made and why it became a bad experience then you are bound to make those same mistakes again.

> **Those who cannot remember the past are condemned to repeat it.**
>
> **—George Santayana, writer and philosopher**

Also, you need to begin to see how your chain of experiences has made you into a complete and different individual from anyone else. This is less true if you are particularly young, in your twenties or earlier, and have always lived in the same city, gone to the same school, and experienced the same activities as your peers. But as you get older and accumulate experiences, these compound and create unique combinations.

By the time you hit your thirties and beyond, you are such a different person from your earlier self and also from anyone else, that it can be hard to grasp. This is the reason why most people never do, and tend to assume that everyone sees the world in a similar way.

As you get older, your path becomes even more disjunct and divergent. Sometimes radically, to the point that your experiences can't really be compared to anyone else. Don't discount this. It seems ordinary to you, because you've lived your life. This can be the source of a unique insight and world view which is all locked up in your experience; all of these are your assets.

Start by collecting a timeline of your life and places you have been, jobs you have had, industries you know. Put those here. You have already worked out some of these by listing skills and education, so don't forget to think about those and write down the experiences related to those.

While there is usually overlap between experience, education and skills, experiences also include good, bad and ugly things you have experienced. It is all important feedback. Make a note of all of those.

Things You Can Do to Find Out What Your Experiences Are

Places you have traveled to.

Hobbies you have or have had.

Places that you have lived in or gone to school. What were your experiences there?

Bad things that have happened to you—those are important as well. What things have failed? What have you been miserable at doing?

From one vantage point life is a continuous stream of experiences from exciting to dull to exciting, from positive to negative and back again. Your life, good, bad or ugly, is defined by the oscillating experiences you have had.

Summary

- Experience is a teacher, but one must be diligent and intentional at learning the lessons.

- The timelines and lists that you have worked on so far, should help you in listing your experiences.

- Don't forget to list the bad things or even ugly things that have happened in your life. You might as well use them and learn the lessons from them.

- Use the questions in The Position to Win, Building A Better Position—Experience questionnaire.

- Go to PositionToWinBook.com to download a printable version of the questionnaire.

POSITION TO WIN

Building a Better Position—Who Are You?

EXPERIENCE

1. Think about your lists of Skills and Education. What experiences are attached to those? This might be a long list. Write a few. You will keep adding them.

_____

_____

2. List the places you have traveled to.

_____

_____

3. Attach the experiences that you have had traveling to these places.

_____

_____

4. Places you have lived in or gone to school.

_____

_____

5. Think about hobbies you have or have had. What are the experiences attached to those?

_____

_____

6. Think about the "bad" experiences that you have had. Try to list some of them here and also why you think those were bad experiences. Why did they fail? What went wrong? Be self-critical. The idea here is to discover things that we need to learn so that things *don't* go bad.

_____

_____

Download this form at https://PositionToWinBook.com

Notes

Chapter 19

Resources

Life is constantly providing us with new funds, new resources, even when we are reduced to immobility. In life's ledger there is no such thing as frozen assets.
—Henry Miller, US author (1891 - 1980)

Innovation is the specific instrument of entrepreneurship...the act that endows resources with a new capacity to create wealth.
—Peter Drucker, *Innovation and Entrepreneurship*, 1985

Few men during their lifetime come anywhere near exhausting the resources dwelling within them. There are deep wells of strength that are never used.
—Richard Byrd, American Naval Officer and explorer (1888 - 1957)

Resources are probably the most underrated assets in people's lives. Not only are they invisible to most, but in the minds of many they are worth little to nothing. Yet knowing and managing your resources can completely change your positioning.

Who do you have contact with and who can you talk to that most people can't? If you think about the concept of "six degrees of separation" you will understand what we are saying.

Chances are that you have access to people in your immediate network that you are discounting who could help you achieve that "pivot" you are looking for.

There are circles within circles of people. You probably know someone who knows someone who you are trying to talk to. The idea here is to list these people as resources so you can aim some of your other positioning artillery toward them.

Also among your resources are things that you own and other tangibles, such as financial resources, specialized machinery or software, perhaps an inheritance or a house in a particular city. List those here.

Things You Can Do To Find Out What Your Resources Are

Think about the previous set of assets, your education and experience and think about the people you know and knew in these different places and activities you were involved with, for example. Write these down.

Things that you own. Things like health, physical attributes and financial resources.

How many hops away are you from getting close to someone who could potentially help you pivot?

Resource List

People:
- Trusted advisors
- Trusted vendors
- Masterminds
- Speakers
- Authors
- Craftsmen
- Experts
- Gurus

Groups /Associations:
- Trade shows
- Conferences

Printed Material:
- Books
- Magazines
- Newspapers
- Photos

Anything Associated With Communications:
- Movies
- Online learning services
- Internet
- Google
- Amazon
- Evernote
- Email lists
- Social media followers
- Blogs
- Articles

Tools:
- **Mechanical:**
- **Mental:**
  - Calculator
  - Computer
  - Software
  - Scanner
  - Smart phone

Systems:
- Processes
- Problem Solutions
- Instructions
- Templates

Financial

Summary

- Make the time and effort to note specifics even when they seem unrelated, not important, or not valuable enough. Many times you can get some truly key insights from seemingly insignificant data.

- Your resources are most likely extremely undervalued by you. Chances are that you don't even see them. Take the time to go over the questions and fill them out completely.

- Go through the Five Dimensions of Personal Positioning and write down some of them following the instructions. The important thing here is to get started to organize and document your assets. Mentally writing them down does not count.

- Use the suggestions on each dimension to come up with things to write. This is not something you do all in one afternoon. Chances are it will take several sessions to come up with ideas in all five dimensions.

- Carry 3 x 5 cards and a fast pen. A slick pen that doesn't stick and writes fast—Pilot G2, for example.

- Use the questions in the Position to Win, Building a Better Position—Resources questionnaire to help you write down what your resources are.

- Go to PositionToWinBook.com to download a printable version of the questionnaire.

POSITION TO WIN

Building a Better Position—Who Are You?

RESOURCES

1. List the people that you know or have come to know through your different experiences, such as the schools you have attended or jobs you have had. Also the hobbies or places that you have traveled. You have probably met people.

_____

_____

_____

2. List the things that you own.

_____

_____

_____

3. List your financial resources.

_____

_____

_____

4. List intangible resources that you have. (health, reputation, fame in a particular area, physical attributes.)

_____

_____

5. How many "hops" are you from "getting to someone" that could potentially help you get to that next pivot?

_____

_____

_____

Download this form at https://PositionToWinBook.com

Notes

Chapter 20

The Seven "Aces" of the Position to Win System

Pocket Aces (a concealed pair of Aces) in Texas Hold'em poker is the best hand out of a possible 169 hands.
—Harsh reality of poker

Aces are larger than life and greater than mountains.
—Mike Caro, professional poker player, pioneer poker theorist and author (1944 -)

Whether you're an Ace as a pilot—top of the heap,
or an Ace in tennis—unreturnable,
Aces exemplify the pinnacle of achievement.
—John Paul Mendocha

I have come a long way from my days as a professional gambler in Vegas. While I no longer live in that world, it taught me many valuable lessons that I still use and that I share with my clients, and now you.

If caught with seven aces in a poker game, feign surprise

Dealing yourself a winning hand means dealing yourself the best cards possible. The best card possible in poker is the Ace.

In poker, when you have an Ace, it not only means that you have a great card but it also means that the other people at the table *don't*; which is just as important.

It also means that if you actually happen to have an Ace and are able to get another one and another one and so on, the power of the cards compound significantly. In poker, if you're ever sitting at a table and there are more than four Aces, the best solution is a 9 mil.

What I learned is that in business and in life, there are actually more than four Aces that you can deal your-

214

self. This is why the *Position to Win System* is structured around seven Aces that together form a cohesive system of positioning to give you the winning hand.

These seven Aces are:

1. Positioning

2. Adoption Curve

3. Marketing Postures

4. Green Field

5. Layer Cake

6. Inciting Incident

7. Sales Funnel

Positioning is the Cornerstone—The First Ace

Positioning is the first Ace, and it is the one that this book is about. If you have read this far, you are at least somewhat acquainted with what positioning is and why it is important. The reason most businesses fail in the first five minutes is that they fail to have a tangible sustainable, defendable position. If you can't answer the question, "What is your positioning statement?" in less than 60 seconds, in all likelihood, you have failed to codify your position.

Bubbly Sugar Water Positioning

If I asked you to name a cola drink most of you will say Coca-Cola. That is because in spite of Pepsi having spent millions of dollars and decades competing with Coke, Coca-Cola is the brand that owns the number one position in the mind of people who drink cola drinks. Once you get that position it is very hard to change people's minds and dislodge that brand.

If you had only one Ace this would be a good one to have. However, it is just the beginning in the *Position to Win System.*

Prove it to Yourself Positioning Test

One of the hardest things about positioning is that it is so ingrained in our heads that we take it for granted. It is very important that you prove to yourself that you can recognize positioning all around you. This happens to me every time I fly. Some years I fly so often when people ask me where I'm from, I say, "Seat seven F." That's a lot of flying. Then the conversation continues and invariably, they ask me what I do. Continuing down the path, we get to marketing, advertising and sales, which is my area of expertise.

That's my opening to bring up a very powerful, important concept called positioning. I refer to the Ries and Trout book on positioning. Over the years, I have run into maybe one or two people of the hundreds I've talked to, who've actually heard of the book.

Ready or Not . . .

When I fly I very often turn to my seat companion and say, "It's time for my favorite game—the Positioning Test. A game where you prove positioning to yourself every single day. This is a test that everyone should take."

Some people hear the word "test" and tighten up, cinch up, get nervous, because they have a little test anxiety. I try to settle them down by saying it's a simple test and no matter what, you will pass and do fine. Now, some of them are enthusiastic and want to begin immediately.

I tell them I'm going to ask a question and the first thing that pops into their head I want them to just blurt

216

it out. When they do, that's their answer. Whatever that answer is, it is valid, because that answer is their reactive answer. That is the trigger answer that's inside of their head. It is sitting there at the very top of the stack of that bias map in their head that we talk about.

So here goes. The first question I usually ask them is to name a facial tissue. In usually less than a second, maybe sometimes even half a second, they say Kleenex. I say that's correct. Now let's move on to question number two. Name a cola drink, and they say Coca-Cola. Understand that this is an interesting dynamic because there are a percentage of people who will say Pepsi Cola. Either one is correct because that's what is in their head.

However, from a positioning diagram standpoint, actually Coca-Cola is number one and Pepsi is number two. There's lots of reasons why they may answer it the way they do, but whatever they say reflects their truth. Then I ask them the third question, which is name a Japanese car company. They say Toyota. Some people will say Honda, but overwhelmingly the answer given is Toyota.

I now tell my fellow air traveler, "Congratulations! You have just passed the positioning test."

By the way, everyone passes the positioning test. It is to illustrate that positioning is all around us. It proves the universality of the concept of positioning and validates it. That it is not some black magic. It is not something that we don't understand or know much about, but is something that we have all experienced. It is embedded in our brains. Once you become aware of this backdrop and how powerful it is, it starts to change your outlook.

Gabe came up with the rest of the quick ten prompts that show what is already inherent in your head. Answer all ten in rapid fire and you are off to a good start with understanding your bias maps. This also shows your age, demographics, financial situation and a myriad of your own series of biases.

1. Name a facial tissue company.

2. Name a cola drink.

3. Name a Japanese car company.

4. Name a city with skyscrapers.

5. Name a country that exports oil.

6. Name an attraction to visit in Paris.

7. Name a city to go gambling.

8. Name a computer company.

9. Name a tall mountain.

10. Name a search engine.

The sixth question is where do people visit when they go to Paris? If you answer the Louvre, its probably because you're artistically oriented. The point of doing the positioning test is that it is designed to show, convince and validate that all positioning is already in place. You've already been using this with every decision you make. You just haven't realized it. And now you can go from doing it subconsciously to doing it consciously and, therefore, apply it to all forms of communications.

Have fun constructing positioning questions but don't be surprised when someone offers up radically different answers than what you expected. That's called an outlier. Their answer reflects their particular biases. When you get an outlier, its not in the fat part of the bell curve.

What About Your Positioning?

I've had many people who when they start asking these same questions to people, become surprised at how easily these questions get answered. Now it gets a little fuzzy when I ask that same question about their personal positioning. "How would you define yourself and your position?"

They usually look at me dumbfoundedly and say, "Wow, I don't know exactly how I would answer that."

To throw them a lifeline, I ask them where they work, the marketplaces they're in, what their interests are and we start to evolve the concept of personal positioning. We could call it your center of the universe.

The power of the positioning test is that it confirms very clearly that positioning exists, is real and ubiquitous. Whether you want to believe it or not, it's always there, and it's an easy way to learn a great deal about people, as they describe their own position or what they view at the top of their position bias maps. These maps are constantly updating.

Death of Positioning at Internet Speeds

I recently talked to Gabe about using Skype to get hold of somebody in Singapore. He cringed at the sound of that because it was so "old school." He glanced at me and said, "Skype? Nobody is on Skype anymore, are you kidding me? Snapchat is bleeding millennial users, too. Only Generation Z are there now."

I said, "Okay, well what's the next step after that?"

"People are using WhatsApp or they're using Facebook Messenger."

Now I had to update inside my own head that the universe had lurched forward to the next minor thing. Skype is gone. We're now over to WhatsApp. In this fast changing world, positioning is becoming more dynamic than it has ever been. But make no mistake—just because it is dynamic doesn't necessarily mean that it is not real and exerts control and power over everything you do. In spite of all the changes there are still people who have AOL email addresses. You almost have to be an anthropologist to use one.

I had to have my Honda Clarity Hydrogen future car towed because rats chewed off the wire to the hydrogen tank. Oh, the Hindenburg of it! Turns out that those little Black Plague bastards did almost $13,000 worth of damage to me driving the future. I used a towing company that the dealer paid for. Jeff did a fantastic job. He said, "Let me give you a card just in case you need us ever again."

I took it. It wasn't until a couple of days later with the card sitting on my kitchen counter that I noticed that they had an AOL email address. Rats destroyed the hydrogen tank, and a man from the 90's showed up to tow the car away! If only we could get an Earthlink account and a Geocities website we could complete the circle of inanity.

Instead of "You've got mail," I'd even sign up again if it said, "You've got rats!"

We all believe a great deal is at stake when we say this is the correct way to do something, because this is how we have it positioned inside of our head. It is etched in those little grey cells. Keep that in mind whenever you're trying to change somebody's mind and get them to do something else.

It is folly to believe that everyone has the same mindset as we do, when, in fact, most of the time, we have no idea what's inside of our head versus what's inside of theirs.

The World's Greatest Motor Sport Spectacular

I just recently mentioned a car race to a client and he was unaware and unimpressed. I love open-wheel auto racing, and had spent several hours watching the Indy 500, known the world over as "The Greatest Spectacle in Racing."

It's the largest attended race in the US and people come from around the world to experience it. Approximately 300,000 people show up every year, and yet the person I was talking to said in a deadpan manner, "Oh, yeah, I think I've heard about that."

That is positioning and bias that exists in his head. People have the backdrop they have. They are predisposed to a certain thought pattern, and in all likelihood, unless you work with that bias instead of trying to blast away at it, you will not be successful dealing with them.

Everyone who has an idea, rushes out to ask people, "What do you think of my cool idea?" Usually they meet people who agree with them because they're their friends or relatives. This gives a skewed opinion of what's actually going on, because you have no idea whether anybody's gonna buy. This is a gross example of a bias group problem.

Speaking slower and louder does not make a foreigner who does not understand your language understand you. Positioning is learning to speak the language of your customer and what is exactly in their head because they have their own language, vocabulary and vernacular, and all of that comes together to build a mind-set. Keep this uppermost in mind as you go forward in selling, advocating and moving your product, service or point of view.

Adoption Curve—The Second Ace

The Adoption Curve describes the rate and process of adoption of an idea or innovation.

The question is always how will my new idea, product or service be received by the market? One must gain an awareness of where one lives on the adoption curve because that informs the type of message and even the channels that one uses to market one's idea. Once you have a position, the first Ace, then you must figure out where you live on the adoption curve. Who are the people who will actually purchase or buy into what you have? That determines how you will sell to them. Positioning drives where you live on the adoption curve.

An example of the adoption curve is when Apple came out with the iPad. Everybody made fun of the name, however it was time for the iPad. It killed this underpowered Netbook, which had been an amazing success story. Everybody and his brother, from Samsung to all the Chinese knock-offs started building imitation Android pads or tablets. The whole tablet market went crazy. The timing was right for Apple. The Netbook was supplanted by better technology.

Raging Verbalist Bests ET and Calls Home

Another great example of the adoption curve is the cellular phone. Year after year people would walk up to me and talk about the miracle of being able to call anybody, anywhere, anytime. Each year, every year, a different crop of adopters would extol the virtues of this seemingly magical device.

As a ridiculously early adopter, I had one bolted into my Chevy Sprint in early 1988—the car had an MSRP of around $8,000 bucks. The bad-ass Motorola phone with the three-watt transmitter was $3,495.00 not including installation. The deal that I had made with Mercury Computer Systems was that if I closed this big deal, they would buy me a cell phone. I code-named that big customer GOLD. The customer loved their code name, and after the sale, I was ecstatic with the commissions and the phone.

Little did I realize that cell phone installers at the time were clueless about maintaining the integrity of my car.

The best location for the antenna was in the center of my roof, and they put an inch and a half hole in it, which to my chagrin, made it look like a radio controlled toy car. I couldn't bitch too much because it had great reception.

For those of you who think your cell phone bills are high, my average bill during that time was $850 a month. I'm too afraid to adjust it for inflation. Even today, there are people who are brand-new to cell phones and the idea of this magic device. The craziest part about it is that it is effectively a radio—that is the underlying technology.

No matter who I talk to, or what age they are, from 8 to 88, they're a little shocked and surprised to hear that, and tell me that I don't know what I'm talking about. It's proof positive that while the technical details matter for functionality, for the end user, they could care less.

Faster Than a Speeding Network

The cellular phone is an example of a concept that became a product that has moved through the entire adoption curve from end to end. Soon there will be more cell phones than there are people. The only people who don't have a cell phone today are either really old, use Jitterbug with very large buttons, conspiracy theorists who are convinced that the radio waves are effecting their brain, or Luddites who stay away from all technology.

Proof of the power of the wave of the adoption curve is that Apple would have never become a one trillion dollar company without the iPhone.

Wherever you are on the adoption curve is going to determine how many sales are left in this market. Not a single client that I have ever encountered has understood where they fit on the adoption curve. They waste significant money on advertising, marketing and sales efforts to the wrong part of the adoption curve.

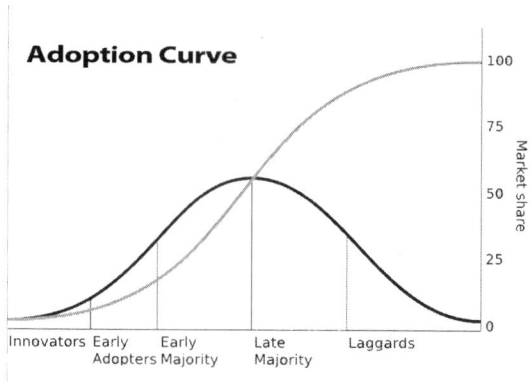

The secret treasure map

The adoption curve is a bell curve, and as you go forth on the curve, you are going to see a deceleration of growth in the market. The midpoint of the bell curve is 50% market penetration. Depending on when you start your business, at that particular time, the interaction between your position and the adoption curve expressing the size and magnitude of the market will define the total available market (TAM). This will have a significant impact and consequence to your success.

Every success depends on you catching the wave of your adoption curve. Miss it, and you'll never catch up to it. Catch it, and you'll rapidly approach the height of unearned marketing genius.

Old School, Like a Bad Smell, is Hard to Get Rid Of

Over the past 20 years, Harvard should have concentrated on building video studios where professors, domain experts, and know-it-alls could disseminate their information to a vast audience for a fraction of the cost of higher education at Harvard and elsewhere. Instead they built buildings and underutilized the Internet.

224

In the last 20 years, people have spent more money on education that at any time in history. We are 1.3 trillion dollars in student loan debt. Institutions should rework higher education. With the Internet you have the ability to take the top minds and have them present, not to a small room of people, but to the entire world.

We Don't Need No Innovation . . .*
*sing to Pink Floyd's *Brick in the Wall*

I'm sitting next to this woman on a flight from Boston to Denver. We start talking about this thing called the Internet. She turns out to be an adjunct professor at Harvard. I said, "Someday in the near future, all of this stuff will be online. And that means, people will be able to get a university degree for significantly less money."

She scoffed, "Harvard's never going to put this stuff online."

There are more cat videos up online than there are Harvard courses. Mr. Muffy Discovers the Yarn Ball has more views than Harvard Law school's online courses.

There's no technological barrier to implement change. Twenty years later, we're still racking up record student loan debt, and we're not having people utilize the technology that's available. We don't appear to be on the road to fixing this problem. We have politicians talking about absolving 1.3 trillion in debt, but no one is speaking about utilizing present day resources and solving the problem. The skills gap has widened in the last 20 years—it has not narrowed.

Today we have all of this capability. We have all of these on demand video services, and we still have a higher education system that's stuck in the 1970's.

Marketing Postures—The Third Ace

The next Ace highlights that even when you know your position and where you live on the Adoption Curve, now you have to develop a plan of attack targeting that section of the market. However, this must be done in the context of the competition. Ignore this at your extreme peril. If you ignore this, you will walk into a minefield and not know what happened when your limbs get blown off.

Everyone wants to be number one. It's almost impossible to look at any media and not see some advertising message with a big giant #1 like that zealot in a football stadium wearing a big foam rubber cowboy hat and two giant #1 foam hands.

They call me Mr. #1

226

Positioning tells us that we can't have 320 million #1's and no # 2's. I had a turnaround client who couldn't accept his position in the marketplace, and he said to me, with his combination Boston/New York accent, "We just gotta be number one."

Unfortunately, from the market's perspective, truth be told, he came up as number none. Like every good consultant playing client golf, I didn't look at him and say, "Don, it ain't gonna happen." Instead, I applied the marketing postures to improve their sales significantly.

The marketing postures as defined in the book, *Marketing Warfare* by Al Ries and Jack Trout, were my starting place for this key Ace. The only problem was that Al and Jack were swimming with the dolphins by the yacht club, while I was down by the dumpster with fingerless gloves, smoking red apple cigarettes with a fire in a used oil drum. That's where real marketing is taking place. Ain't no co-efficients down there.

You either seriously fight it out, or you're going to get your head handed to you. All Al and Jack said was true, but they left about 70% out of it. So let me clear it up for anybody's who not running a Fortune 500 company.

For most of your career, you would be better served to follow a three word piece of advice:

Put simply, few have the luxury to sit around and pontificate when they need to be out there in the jungle avoiding the napalm from the sky; building

tunnels that the tanks don't collapse; and winning the deals that you can. The likelihood of you being successful will increase immeasurably if you understand what posture will work for you.

Just like positioning, your marketing posture depends on context—the context of your resources and of the competition. Learn what your posture should be so you make the best use of your resources and more importantly, not get killed!

The 4 Marketing Postures:

Defensive Posture

Offensive Posture

Flanking Posture

Guerrilla Posture

Posture	Who Qualifies
1. Defensive	Only one—the Top Dog
2. Offensive	Only one or two big dogs the second or third big players in the market
3. Flanking	Two to five mid-size dogs Size dictates what you can or can't do—has to be a big enough company to out-flank somebody
4. Guerilla	All the rest of the mutts

Know where you fit

Green Field—The Fourth Ace

Look at the landscape and find a new field

This is an Ace that describes the process by which you can divide a market, find a niche, sub-niche, mini-niche, micro-niche, nano-niche, pico-niche or itty-bitty-niche as a new market that doesn't exist. How can you find the new open, unspoiled Green Field even if your innovation isn't entirely new?

Ride hailing services like Uber and Lyft came to age because they figured out the timing of the intersectionality of technology and market desire for them to exploit the ability to connect people to each other to get a ride.

It is not new, yet it *is* because it was a Green Field.

What is a Green Field?

All businesses reside in a market and most markets are crowded affairs—think the Tokyo subway. Innovation is finding a place, a hole, a pocket that is not over-inhabited. That is a Green Field.

Why is a Green Field necessary?

When you put your value proposition out into the marketplace, you will gain one of three reactions:

1. Not interested—a giant head slap of negativity.

Don't feel too special at this reaction, considering that there are more people in the United States who have not been to Starbucks than who have.

2. Ambivalent—this is the worst place to be.

They don't care whether they buy from you or someone else. There is little to no differentiation. It is this middle ground that is the road to commoditization and with it, a race to the bottom for pricing, quality, and brand loyalty.

3. WOW—an excitement and sense of wonderment.

Green Field is all about differentiation, uniqueness and breakthroughs. There is a rush by the early adopters who want to be the first to capture the magic. They are possessing something new. Green Fields are important because if the solution that fits this market space explodes, it will wipe out other solutions in neighboring markets.

You have to be careful that you don't have on the wrong colored glasses and think its a green field when it's a brown dusty desert.

My Death Certificate Read
Cause of Death—Power Point

My recurring nightmare is that I'm sitting in a room, and I know I've probably descended to Dante's Inferno, because there is a continuous stream of dull, boring pitches about derivative, me-too, uninspired businesses. This is worse than any zombie movie, because at least zombies want to kill you quickly and eat your flesh instead of killing you slowly syllable by syllable. Starry eyed business owners drone on, unable to articulate their position, their adoption curve, their posture, and instead of having a clear green field, they're living in the delusional world of unicorns, cotton candy trees and a rainbow bridge.

The worst of them have carefully crafted many hundreds of slides in the deck, to which they have painstakingly figured out a mauve, forest green and mustard yellow palette. In the dream all I want to do is escape their presentation as the whirling projector fan sounds like a bad bowling alley. When they notice my disdain for their lack of originality, they tell me, "But wait till you see our magical, made up numbers which grow to the sky."

Jack's Magic Beans have nothing on them. They show that in just a few short years, they will be staring at a billion dollar valuation on the precipice of greatness with not an original molecule of a thought between them.

I try to wake up from this nightmare because I realize that they're pitching me to become their consultant and take them to the "Promised Land" of unlimited funding, easy to get customers, and no delays in their development schedule. My eyes open rapidly, I sit up in bed sweating, check my phone, and realize that the meeting is six hours away.

These meetings are repeated hundreds if not thousands of times a day, from Starbucks to WeWork to a hotel room, and it appears none of them understand that the most important thing they need in all of this hyper-competitive world is what every dog needs—a green field.

Layer Cake—The Fifth Ace

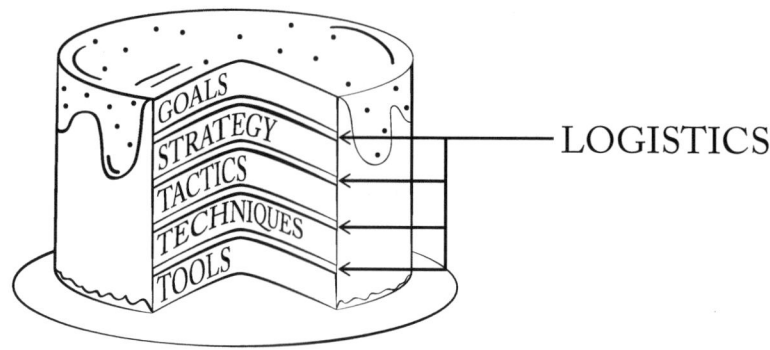

GOALS
STRATEGY
TACTICS
TECHNIQUES
TOOLS

LOGISTICS

Demystifying business hierarchy

What is a Layer Cake?

The layer cake is a hierarchical structure. A systematic way of prioritizing action that aligns with stated goals. It is the means by which you filter and order the innumerable tasks that are actually needed. Along with that, and just as importantly, it helps you define all the things that you should not do, not buy, or not build.

The layer cake is a means to unconfuse the various levels of understanding how businesses and organizations function. It is very easy to tell people all they have to do is to set goals and they are well on the way to achieving them.

Unfortunately, the current dogma is that goals are almost sacrosanct. This charade is further promulgated by bogus studies that purport to show that those who write out goals achieve significantly more than those who don't. Duh.

I used to drink from this simplistic Kool-Aid punch bowl, only to become discouraged when things didn't turn out like I thought they should. Back to the drawing board.

The pundit said what you need is positive thinking and visualization. No matter how much I focused my brain waves on the phone—it never rang. Something was missing. As I became more successful and shed the naive pablum of the cult of goal setters, it became clear that no hole was going to exist unless somebody took a shovel, put some sweat into it, and started digging.

Clearly there are such things as goals, but just like the top of a layer cake, there has to be something underneath it. Currently, I believe that any goal that can be obtained must be supported by the foundational layers that support the aspirations of the goal.

Once this insight became clear to me, it meant that I needed to find what the other layers were. This is not a theoretical process; I have back-checked it through many clients and business situations. The layer cake should provide you with a significant advantage, and more importantly show you where the deficiencies lie.

The layer cake is a construct that allows you to swiftly understand whether or not you have the necessary support to obtain the desired end goal. It is rapid and acutely accurate. The layer cake will save you a great deal of grief, stress, and money. Further, it is a means of commonality with any sized project from a one piece band to a 120 piece orchestra.

It will get you out of the habit of buying tools that don't connect with your stated purpose and allows you to focus on the strategies that *will* be used to accomplish your goals.

The layer cake constantly answers these questions and tells you where specifically an item is, using positioning and context. What tools do you need to use? What techniques do you need to master? How do you put them into tactical order that supports a given strategy to accomplish said goal?

If you don't have a way, a means of structuring concepts and putting them together in a coherent fashion, you will get confused, and a confused mind always says, "No."

Do you ever feel like you showed up, and everything was off just a little bit? This happens quite often in life. I was in the process of delivering a speech and I noticed a young guy, we'll call him Charlie, who was feverishly taking notes. Even from the stage, I knew I'd never get out of the room alive.

Sure enough, as I exited the stage, I spied Charlie making a beeline for me, dragging his bag while frantically throwing everything together. As he reached me, clutching his belongings, he says, "Incredible speech. I really connected with you."

An overstatement to say the least, because I hadn't spoken a single syllable to him directly. Hand extended, he shook mine vigorously. He asked immediately if he could buy me breakfast, lunch, dinner, a cup of coffee—just ten minutes of my precious time.

I had been speaking long enough to be on guard for the Charlies of the world. I said, "Lets start with coffee before we decide on the monograms for the towels."

Close Encounters of a Strategy Kind

He was elated, so off we went towards the Starbucks. First, I had to stop off at the men's room, and I suggested that I may need a moment of quiet contemplation. He waited anxiously out in the hall. At Starbucks he had his loyalty card ready. I ordered my usual Vente Decaf Americano with an extra shot of decaf, with a little room.

He was surprised that I was this energetic and not caffeinated. I found a table and as I was sitting down someone else from the conference noticed me and started walking quickly towards me. Charlie abandoned his credit card at the counter, whisked over to the table and told the intruder that he'd already purchased a cup of coffee for me and that this was going to be a private conversation.

After obtaining the coffee, Charlie sat down, looked at me with that enough-chit-chat-let-me-tell-you-my-great-idea look. In the course of the next agonizing 850 seconds he used the word strategy once every 14 seconds. He had what I would call a word fetish—that kinky, twisted brain that loves the word strategy.

St-RAT-egy

If you stand back and look at the word strategy, it has the word rat embedded in it. I felt like I was in a fog because clearly, though he loved the word all dressed up in high heels, he had no idea what it meant and he never said a single thing that was actually a strategy.

I kept waiting for him to need a breath, but apparently, his alien lungs with exceptional capacity, fluttered over his vocal chords allowing him to continue to spew forth the word strategy unabated.

Hoping that he was going to wind down, like a kid's toy running out of steam, I threw the only life-line I had, "Your coffee is getting cold." It disrupted him for just a brief moment, and as he reached for a sip, I uttered these words, "I developed this construct that allows me to categorize where something fits. It works surprising well in the business world. I call it The Layer Cake."

I produced a sheet of paper, drew out the 5 layers, wrote my name and copyright on it, and suggested that he take another run at his presentation with this new understanding.

He jumped up and exclaimed that this was "Brilliant! Brilliant!" and that this would make his strategy even stronger. Gripping his new found talisman, he walked off triumphantly. I breathed a sigh of relief. I had escaped from the clutches of the Strategy Man. I didn't need a strategy. I needed to quit drinking coffee with guys who rapidly approached me at the stage.

The Layer Cake is a quick and accurate way to understand that you need all five layers to be successful in any business. The power of this Ace is that it allows you to cut through the fog and clutter of those who will want to attempt to bamboozle you with bullshit.

It will make your life significantly more understandable and should prevent you from getting stuck in the wrong place.

The Inciting Incident—The Sixth Ace

I was a Boy Scout when I was growing up, and was always encouraged to get merit badges—a good way to get knowledge of a certain subject. You get a small booklet usually about 40 or 50 pages, big text, lots of pictures that describe some of the things that take place in that particular area of study.

Once you have the booklet, then you ask your scoutmaster, who happened to be my father, to help you locate one of the people who has expertise in that area. This specialist will then guide you through learning the material. Then you take a test to see if you qualify for the merit badge. One of the merit badges that I achieved was Firemanship. It changed over time to be called Fire Safety.

Firemanship Merit Badge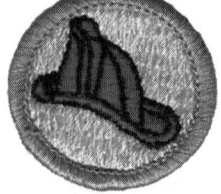

I was about 12-years-old and became excited as I read through the book, because I would be able to talk to a real fireman. He told me a lot about what it takes to deal with a fire: what kind of equipment they use, all the gear they wear and carry, and the adrenaline rush when they are called to a fire.

The amazing lesson I learned, is that homo sapiens, our entire species, was changed radically when we harnessed this thing called fire. Now make no mistake, fire is one of the most destructive things that we have on this planet. Uncontrolled, it burns down forests, destroys habitats, ruins houses, and brings about death and destruction. But we've learned how to control it to an amazing extent. What's interesting is that fire, fundamentally, is made up of only three components. You need:

1. Fuel.

2. Oxygen.

3. Heat.

As a Boy Scout, to start a fire, you have to work really hard. There are three methods: flint and steel,

magnifying glass and friction from bow and spindle. Put the three components in the correct ratio and you can start a fire. I worked an incredibly long time with the bow and spindle method and after a lot of sweat and tears, I started a fire.

The Spark That Changes Everything

Fire is essential to life as we know it. It changed the way we ate. We went from eating raw foods to cooked foods, making it easier to digest and extract the nutrients and minerals.

There is a useful gadget called a PowerPot V that will use a flame under a pot of water that creates enough electricity to charge your smart phone if you are out camping in the wilderness and are having phone withdrawal.

What we can learn most from fire and what I learned at that young age, is that fire, at its core, changed everything. So many things are based upon very fundamental elements put together in the right and proper way. That's what drove me to look for these types of elements in business, sales, marketing, and advertising. I have used the ideas in improving systems in organizations.

Fire teaches us a lot. When you're looking for what you want to accomplish in life, or to build and grow your business, ask yourself what are those fundamental elements that you need to put in place.

Being a Firestarter

The motivation for writing *Position to Win System* was to share how to harness the power of the seven Aces. Some people have low ambition, others have no ambition, or maybe some ambition, or a ton of ambition, but all of us have to deal with how big a fire you want to build; do you want to build a small one, a medium one, a big one, a massive one? And what do you want to do with it? How do you attain enough energy to drive to where you want to go?

When you ask yourself these fundamental questions and you start to build that massive inferno that fills you with ambition, resolve and desire that will encompass your life, you will accomplish more than you ever thought possible. Once you start asking yourself these questions, once you start driving to those points, what you'll find is that winning is one of the most important things in life.

But winning, just like fire, is based upon foundational laws. Once you understand them and apply them, it doesn't mean that you're always going to get the result that you want. Believe me, because the air is so thin, trying to start a fire above timberline with a rainstorm is almost impossible. But you have to figure out how to do it.

Consequently, you learn how to deal with the situation around you and not let circumstances prevent you from getting to that result. Understand that all of us want to know how to get the best result possible. Remember, fire changed everything. Does the fire burn bright inside of you? Can you kindle that energy and that enthusiasm and excitement? If you can, you will change the rest of your life.

Nothing happens until there is a spark, a bolt of lightning that makes the fire. Something clicks, something starts moving forward.

Knowing your inciting incident means that you will quit wasting time with situations that don't have that energy, that intensity, that fire.

Fire changed the way human development took place. Understanding your inciting incident is an Ace that will change the way your business development takes place.

You will focus on what actually moves the needle and what creates that momentum.

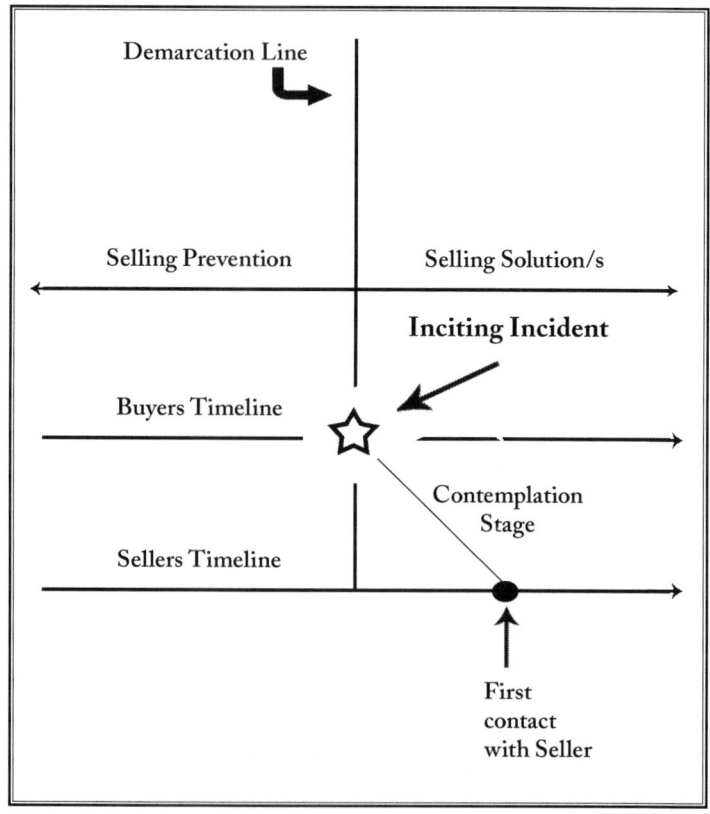

Inciting Incident

The inciting incident is the crisis that drives change. This is the star that you see on the chart to the left on the Demarcation Line. Everything to the left of the Demarcation Line is prevention—everything to the right is the solution or solutions provided by the seller. When you experience an inciting incident, something bad happens that changes the trajectory of the buyer. It could be biological, societal, or emotional, but it's a problem of magnitude.

No one cares about the solution until they have a problem. After the inciting incident, there is a contemplation stage or delay that occurs between the inciting incident and the first contact with the seller who may or may not have the solution.

We are all reaction machines. Over the course of history, we have learned to react to the circumstances and situations around us. These reactions drive us. When one starts to think about how to go about convincing somebody to do something, we need to get their attention. Getting someone's attention, of course, is a reaction to some stimulus that we provide. We provide the stimulus, they react, and then hopefully pay attention.

A Whisper in a Hurricane

So what is missing when one is selling in the marketplace and no one notices? Say we come up with a cool idea, an insight, something that will break through this marketplace maze. We believe people will see what we're talking about no matter what. Unfortunately, that is not the case.

In fact, many ill-conceived ideas are designed that were going to sell prevention.

But something has to happen to wake people up. Prevention is almost impossible to sell.

You have a dinner party planned.

Everything is working out just fine. Friends are coming over, you've had the carpets cleaned, the food is prepared, you've bought the extra bag of ice, and you feel like everything is well in hand.

One of the things that you'll never see on the checklist, is, is the toilet going to back up? Four hours before the party's about to begin, seemingly in an innocuous way, said toilet doesn't perform its appointed duties. And even though a guy named Crapper invented it, you'll understand one thing, you now have a serious problem.

You pull the handle. The water is rising. You stand there in disbelief, because once you pull the handle you never want to see the contents again. You're in a regifting situation.

You immediately go into panic mode, start searching the web for a plumber because even though it wasn't a problem before, its now a serious problem. That is an inciting incident.

P.S. One solution is to convince your party goers to use the bucket.

When Reality Hits the Fan

The inciting incident speaks directly to that. Sellers are on one track and buyers are on the other, they're parallel tracks. They only converge when an inciting incident alerts the buyer that something has to change. They change their trajectory, look at their options, and then engage. There is no other way to do it. So the next time you start thinking about where you fit in the food chain, ask yourself, what is the inciting incident that motivates them to look at your solution. It is tied directly into positioning because without an inciting incident, there is no urgency to seek a solution.

Think about it. We have biological needs that take

place. Urgency is driven when we sit there and say, "Wow, it's 1:00 and I haven't even stopped for lunch." That's an inciting incident. What's the next thing you should do? Get something to eat. The saying never go to a grocery store hungry is absolutely true. Talk about an inciting incident. Your emotions will overcome any logic. You can say, "I'm going to be on the wagon and not buy those crazy chips that I consume by the bagful." We've all been there, very few of us escape. We buy the chips anyway. The inciting incident is just that event that causes us to take action immediately. Without it, we go along the path that we're already on.

My favorite Cavett Roberts quote is, "Can you sustain your enthusiasm long after the initial excitement has died down?" Sounds like he was talking about a fire.

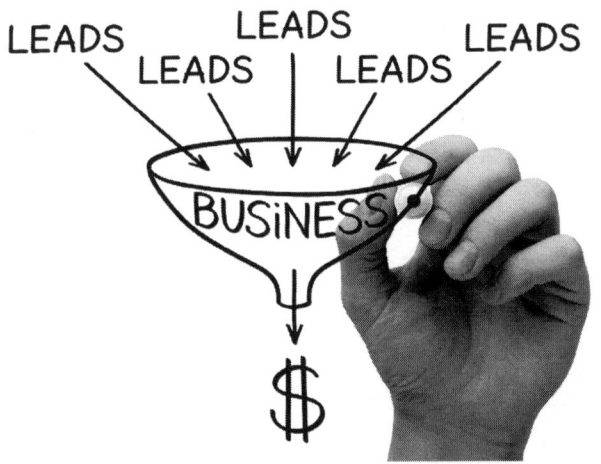

Leads into Gold

Sales Funnel—Ace Number 7

Once you have internalized and applied these six Aces that compound and tilt the odds in your favor, now you will use all of this to set up your Sales Funnel. Or how I like to call it, the sales process, for those of us from the Jurassic period. This will give you the greatest amount of leverage of your time, money and resources.

What is a Sales Funnel?

Every business rests upon the Rat Brain of Business, which is the transaction. Every turnaround I have been involved in fundamentally had a dysfunctional transaction system and did not pay heed to the three simple steps that make up the Rat Brain of Business. They are:

1. Move it from our shelf

2. To their shelf

3. And get paid

The sales funnel is an incorporation of the six Aces into a coherent process that systematically sifts, sorts, and moves from lead to the close and completes the transaction.

Most businesses underestimate the number of steps, effort, and cost to move someone through the funnel. The six Aces provide you with the necessary insights to create an effective, respectable sales funnel—your seventh Ace.

Most of the time when people talk about a sales funnel, what they are and how to build them, they are really talking about some useful tactics, at best. At worst, they are implementing gimmicky tools that don't really help the business at all.

These are your seven steps, your seven Aces of the *Position to Win System*. Every time you add one and work at honing it, it will compound and you will have a better hand. Why not deal yourself these Aces?

Summary

- The *Position to Win System* has 7 Aces that are layers and dimensions of a successfully positioned business, product, service or idea.

- The 7 Aces of the *Position to Win System* are:
  - Positioning
  - Adoption Curve
  - Marketing Postures
  - Green Field
  - Layer Cake
  - Inciting Incident
  - Sales Funnel

- In Poker as in life, the more Aces that you have, the better. The power of each Ace compounds and increases your advantage by understanding not only what your position is, but also by showing where you fit in the Adoption Curve and what your Marketing Posture attack should be. You will be that much better poised to take advantage of the Green Field you happen to be in or are moving towards; the Layer Cake will help you connect the dots of what needs to be done, and the Inciting Incident will sharpen your message.

- Do all of this and integrate it into a cohesive Sales Funnel and your sales process will enjoy an unfair advantage over your competition.

- Go to PositionToWinBook.com/freestuff for more resources.

Notes

Chapter 21

The Fork in the Road:
Are you going to let things happen randomly, or will you Position to Win?

Alice asked the Cheshire Cat, who was sitting in a tree,

What road do I take?

The cat asked, Where do you want to go?

I don't know, Alice answered.

Then, said the cat, it really doesn't matter, does it?

—Lewis Carroll, *Alice's Adventures in Wonderland, 1865*

I have recommended the book, *Positioning: the Battle for Your Mind*, to countless people and have given out several hundred copies of it during my career. I suggest you read it, too. Just as I recommended it to Gabe, when he was a coaching client of mine, before we became partners.

If you have read it or if you eventually read it, you might end up agreeing with Gabe. When he read it, he found out that many of the concepts related to positioning that I have developed over the years are not found in that book. They are not found in any book until the one you are holding in your hands, as a matter of fact.

We then went on to structure a system called Position to Win, that contained what I believed were all the essential pieces in positioning that I have been getting paid six figures a year to develop in different industries over my career as a consultant.

If you don't know yourself, have a level of awareness of your five dimensions of personal positioning, have never gone through a process of self-acceptance and never had a willingness to discover all aspects about yourself, you will resist positioning and succumb to the temptation of delusion.

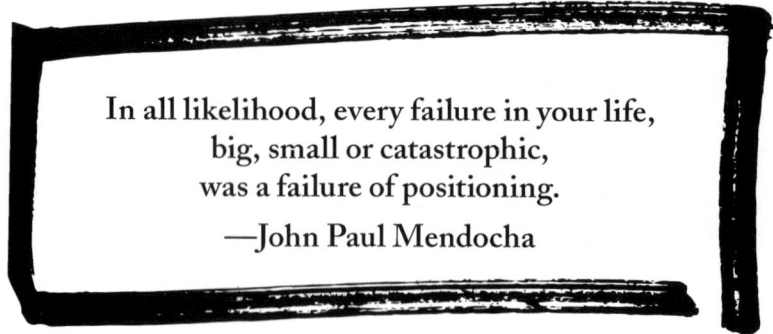

In all likelihood, every failure in your life,
big, small or catastrophic,
was a failure of positioning.
—John Paul Mendocha

Chapter 21: The Fork in the Road

There is no obstacle if you position yourself because you continually move towards something better. There are varying speeds of moving forward. Focus on taking positive action.

Setting a goal that runs counter to your position, however, will in all likelihood, become a very negative thing for several reasons. First, because you won't achieve it. Second, because you will grow frustrated and you will burn valuable time never getting there.

The *Position to Win System* is all about context. From that context you know what you can and cannot work with. Without that context, without that map, you are in the dark and will continuously be lost, wasting time. You will set goals that you are not positioned for and will probably never achieve.

The *Position to Win System* will make your life more successful because it will define and map the things you can capture and then move beyond.

How can you have a winning hand in life, career and business? Apply the seven steps of the *Position to Win System* to anything you want to be successful. You can apply it to decision-making, investing, communications, and any situation where you need to persuade people.

There are six defined areas where you can use positioning—from your personal position to an idea, concept, market, product, and service. You can use it in all kinds of circumstances in business, and any marketing advocating a position. In addition, anything you want to improve in your personal life can be done through positioning.

On the television show *Shark Tank*, the Sharks want to know the sales of the companies they may be willing to invest in. Of greater importance is the position the business enjoys.

Tell me what business you are in, what your market is, but also tell me your defensible position in that market.

The solar panel energy industry is advocating a position as an alternative energy source which they assert is better than fossil fuels.

Al Bundy when asked why we threw tea in Boston harbor, quipped, "Americans don't drink tea—they drink coffee." He was advocating for coffee in the marketplace.

Positioning is not just advertising. With the *Position to Win System* you can organize and understand the dynamics of all life and business situations.

Action Surmounts All Obstacles

If you do nothing else, go out and apply what you have read so far in this book. You can greatly improve where you are and where you are going by understanding your own positioning, and going through the process of honing that better position that you can pivot to.

But if you are, in fact, ready to take the next step in positioning and want to have a deeper understanding of not only that Ace but all seven of them in the *Position to Win System*; if you want to benefit from the experience of over thirty-five years of working with Fortune 500 companies, combined with the experience of my co-author who is in charge of spending hundreds of thousands of dollars a month in online advertising, all put into a cohesive seven-step system where you can have our help, then I suggest you head over to PositionToWinBook.com/free-stuff, and check out the resources.

The sense that one must use everything in this book can become overwhelming. Better to focus and achieve than attempt to do it all. Today, more than ever, there seems to be a race against the sun to see if we can make it all our own. This appears to be a losing hand.

Winners understand that you should always play the hand in front of you to the best of your ability, and then your best will always be in front of you.

We are surrounded by insurmountable opportunities.
—Pogo

Summary

- In all likelihood, every failure in your life has been a failure of positioning. The decision is, will you work on your positioning consciously or will you end up letting chance decide what your positioning will be?

- If you don't know where to go, any road will take you there.

- The *Position to Win System* is structured in a way that you are always improving your position—it moves and evolves as your environment changes.

- Position yourself to win and move around any obstacle.

- If you are ready to take the next step in positioning yourself, go to PositionToWinBook.com

Launching the Book
Vegas Style

It is sometimes said that without a deadline, nothing would get done. Nothing could be truer in the writing of this book. Because of some fever-dream, I looked at my calendar and said, "Let's launch this book, in some shape or form, by FreedomFest 2019, July, 17-20, in Las Vegas."

When you make these bold predictions, you always feel like you have plenty of time. Feeling a little bit like President John F. Kennedy talking about getting somebody to the moon, that July date seemed very far away. Little did I know how much toil would go into this tome.

Having a great team is the only way we made the deadline. This could be a cautionary tale, a chalk outline on the ground, a beware of dragons ahead, but we all forged forward:

John, Gabe, Rebecca, Lyn, Dannelle, and Michael

And I forgot . . . the collaborator of the universe, Murphy, because Murphy always rides for free.

Listing all of the trials and tribulations would require me to put further warnings and potentially various hot-lines in this section, but suffice it to say, there were many.

So as we toiled away at this book, chipping away detail by detail, making compromises, we became determined that we would have an advance reader copy and that we'd have it for FreedomFest, 2019. The best news was that no one, other than the team and my brother Michael, knew that FreedomFest would be the launchpad for this book. Talk about a stealth approach. We had four days of potential promoting, pitching, tap-dancing, jawing, and convincing. We built a Book-Worthy list of those who would attend that we would give the book to.

We enlisted the help of BookBaby to print and ship the books. We missed our deadline by exactly one day, and lost 25% of our promotional window. Starting this process months before, I was determined that this book would not look like some half-baked, poorly put together, self-published piece of shit.

We worked tirelessly to that end, and knew that every person we walked up to, would be the ultimate judge, jury and potential executioner.

I ordered 100 books, 25 of which would be shipped overnight, (expensive—books are heavy), and three additional boxes of 25 books each, that would arrive later. Doing something that most professional advice givers never do, we took our own advice and built marketing pieces: an oversized postcard and business cards. Once you launch that missile, the schedule is basically locked and loaded.

Gabe, Michael and I arrived in Vegas with business cards, postcards, and smiles.

While handing out the material, the first ah-hah moment hit—even though the title was *Position to Win,*

Epilogue: Launching the Book Vegas Style

Most Businesses Fail in the First 5 Minutes, It Just Takes Them 3-5 Years to Realize It, like a magnet drawing another magnet, people's eyeballs hit on the words Most Businesses Fail in the First 5 Minutes and they were verbalizing and nodding in agreement. Even without the book, that became the conversation starter.

I handed out the material, I told them the books were arriving the next day. Several said they were not going to be there, but were fascinated, none the less. First day mission accomplished—we established a basic pitch and rhythm. That night, I checked the UPS tracking number every couple of hours, waiting for our precious cargo to appear.

Waking up early, Gabe and I were ecstatic that the first box had arrived at UPS, and that we could pick it up at 9 a.m. Think of it as a delayed Christmas morning. We drove over to UPS, arriving early. Several vehicles were already parked in the lot, but no one was waiting at the door; we were the first in line.

In less than 15 minutes, I went from someone who always wanted to write a book, to holding one in my hands. It felt fantastic. Never again would I hear from someone, "You should write a book."

We drove back over to Paris, the Vegas resort, not the city in France, shared the great news with Michael, and then got serious about getting people interested in the book.

Over the next few days, we gave the book to people from my Book-Worthy list, and I only missed two. The response was better than I could have expected. Before long, it became obvious, that the title would have to be changed, because everyone said, "Most businesses fail in the first 5 minutes—talk to me about that."

Two video interviews ensued, excitement was building, and I established a new rule: never go anywhere without a copy of the book.

I continued to give out copies to those who were Book-Worthy. I talked to Evelyn Brady-Watters, an entrepreneur who was just starting a business and a potential opportunity for me; and Matthew Taylor, the winner of a film festival award. As I handed him a copy of the book and signed it with a Sharpie, he looked at his wife and said, "This guy knows what he's doing, he's got a Sharpie."

Book-Worthy list (in no particular order)

Greg Writer

Glenn Beck

Heather Wagenhals

Jim Woods

Erin Brownback

Herman Cain

Mark Skousen

Kevin Harrington

Jon D. Fondy

Dr. Warren Farrell

George Gilder

Michael Holdmann

Nicolas Tomboulides

Naomi Brockwell

Evelyn Brady-Watters

Mathew Taylor

Sandra Haack

Epilogue: Launching the Book Vegas Style

Mark Eliot

Dave VanHoose

Jonathan and Dawn Stone

Chris Rabalais

James Brown

Robert Lawson

As we reflected upon the lessons learned from the launch, the goals of making this look, feel, and be a real book had been achieved. However, we needed to finish it all the way, which is what you hold in your hands today—the finished product.

Notes

About the Authors

John Paul Mendocha

I have been a busy guy. Instead of going to college, I went to Las Vegas and became a professional gambler in the School of Hard Knocks. Which, of course, didn't prepare me for anything in the corporate world but at the same time it prepared me for anything.

I went on to work in High Tech which allowed me to do something that no one in my family lineage had done— become a millionaire. I got a job at Mercury Computer Systems, which right now is worth between eight hundred million and one billion. When I started selling product we told everyone we were doing four million, which was a stretch. In 1989, I put them on the INC 500 in position number eighteen!

This led to me becoming a turnaround specialist with twenty turnarounds on my resume and counting.

Three books that I recommend to all my clients

On every *Positioning The Battle for Your Mind* book that I give away, I write—Position yourself as a winner!

About the Authors

Gabe Bautista

I am originally from Bogotá, Colombia growing up in the "Narcos" era in a society surrounded by the violence of the cartels and the ensuing civil war that has torn the country for decades. I moved to the United States in my adolescence, carrying with me stories with happy endings and others not so much.

Music was my first love which led me to become a classically trained composer. I still write and play the piano daily. I eventually found my way to business and consulting. How could music have prepared me for business? Turns out very well, in fact!

My first client was the music school where I was teaching. That's where I started my first pivot out of music, helping them with systems, hiring, training, integrating technology, teaching and more. I left that job and started working with marketing agencies, eventually getting hired as a third party to work with difficult digital advertising accounts.

Later I went out on my own and companies hired me to devise their digital growth strategy and structure the implementation of Google advertising, Facebook advertising, social media and all things digital. It was then that I started to be able to use not only my digital expertise but found myself fixing sales process problems, system problems and logistics.

That's when I started working with John Paul Mendocha, first as a coaching client, being mentored by John Paul, and finally becoming business partners doing business turnarounds, and now as co-author of *Most Businesses Fail in the First 5 Minutes, It Just Takes Them 3 to 5 Years to Realize It.*

Bibliography

Positioning: The Battle for Your Mind by Al Ries and Jack Trout

Diffusion of Innovation by Everett Rogers

Marketing Warfare by Al Ries and Jack Trout

Managing Oneself by Peter F. Drucker

The Essential Drucker by Peter F. Drucker

The Effective Executive by Peter F. Drucker

The Art of War by Sun Tzu

Special thanks to:

Al Ries and Jack Trout

Everett Rogers

Peter F. Drucker

Sun Tzu

Acknowledgments

Writing a book is *very* hard.

My wife Rebecca Ann (Mertus) Mendocha

My brother Michael R. Mendocha

My Parents—sadly long gone

    Margaret Anna (Ronne) Mendocha

    Chester Walter Mendocha

Dan Gordan—Lifetime best friend

Rick Morgan—Best business partner and friend

Big Joe Kraus—Mentor, friend and best boss
(miss you everyday)

Gabe Bautista—Co-conspirator

Murray Egan—Knowing the terminal velocity of a
1989 Olds Cutlass Ciera

Perry Marshall—My younger brother from another
mother

Tom Meloche—In your hollowed out volcano

Doug Wilmarth—Patient zero

Dan Kennedy—A huge change in trajectory

Duncan MacIntyre—The Iron Man

John Montelione—I banged on the door
and he opened it.

—John Paul Mendocha

Acknowledgments

I want to acknowledge the structure of reality,
which inexorably has brought me here.
I really mean it,
thank you,
for all of it.

I would like to acknowledge my mother and brother—whose quiet but incessant support have been an ongoing fuel for me—you motivate me. Also my uncle and aunt together with my cousin who all together constitute my entire family; you are those who have believed in me from day one, and have shown me your support and love even at my worst times.

To John Paul, whom I deeply respect and who has trusted me with his time and energy—here's to many more projects together.

I would also like to thank someone very special but I know she would prefer that I leave her name out. Thank you for all the simple and beautiful moments you gave me. Even while writing part of this book in Rome, I remember looking up and seeing you there and smiling, I won't forget those moments and all I learned. I'll keep them with me always.

I feel thankful for the opportunity to grow in ever more nuanced and heightened self-awareness and gratitude, so that what was once pain, addiction, abuse, anxiety, depression and darkness, may turn to kindness, positivity and hope.

—Gabe Bautista

Collectively, In No Particular Order . . .

Without your sense of adventure we would have never gotten this done this fast:

Position to Win System—Beta Program:

Bill Farinella

Dike Drummond

Richard Duggal

Sara Davis

Dominick DeJoy

Doug Wesney

Philip Meese

Luigi Gonzalez

Victor Glavan in Rome, Italy. For helping us out with the Italian errands with great generosity

Duncan MacIntyre for his research prowess and assistance, the Iron Man

Lyn Adelstein—Muse and graphic design specialist

Dannelle Hollinshead—Personal Assistant, unwavering effort through difficult tasks

Most Businesses Fail in the First 5 Minutes

Index

A

Most Businesses Fail in the First 5 Minutes

You're at the fork in the road.

This is not a dream and you sure as hell aren't Alice talking to the Cheshire Cat.

If this were the case, I might suggest there are other more pressing problems.

But you ARE here, and you've made it to the end of the book.

CONGRATULATIONS!

You've read the book, but you now realize you've simply just begun your journey down the rabbit hole of POSITIONING and you still have some questions as to where to go next.

Without knowing your positioning, it's a lot like not knowing where you want to go.

If you don't know where you're going, any road will do.

And who wants to be listening to advice from a cat anyways, especially one that is fueled by LSD?

Besides, the bridge to nowhere is traveled heavily enough.

Seeing that you've gone this far, you're not interested in that path.

Neither was Doug. Because of the *Position To Win System,* he was able to position his team for million dollar projects that other people wanted to take credit for.

He not only set up his team for recognition but solidified his position to fend off his ruthless competition! He got the long sought promotion and ultimate success.

What about you?

Do you know your position and how to defend it?

Entering Alice's Wonderland required a change in the state of Caroll's conscience.

Positioning, too, is a mindset.

If you're ready to go further down the rabbit hole of success and are prepared to engage in the battle for your mindset on positioning, then go to the link below for FREE access to ALL the resources listed in the book:

PositionToWinBook.com/FreeStuff

If you're NOT ready to succeed, do NOT even THINK about starting down this rabbit trail...

But if you ARE ready, well, welcome to the journey!

It's only just begun and it's going to be a wild ride, so HOLD ON TIGHT!

John Paul Mendocha and Gabe Bautista

Lewis Caroll (Charles Lutwidge Dodgson) is the author of *Alice's Adventures in Wonderland.*